EDUCATION MATTERS

General Edi

SPECIAL E

D0247518

BOOKS IN THIS SERIES

SPECIAL
EDUCATION
Jonathan Solity

CASSELL

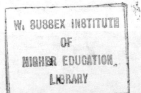

Cassell Educational Ltd
Villiers House, 41/47 Strand, London WC2N 5JE
378 Park Avenue South, New York, NY 10016–8810

First published 1992

British Library Cataloguing-in-Publication Data
A catalogue record for this book is available from the British Library

Library of Congress Cataloging-in-Publication Data
Available from the Library of Congress

ISBN 0–304–32407–8 (hardback)
0–304–32427–2 (paperback)

Phototypeset by Intype, London
Printed and bound in Great Britain by
Biddles Ltd, Guildford and King's Lynn

CONTENTS

FOREWORD

Professor E. C. Wragg, Exeter University

During the 1980s a succession of Education Acts changed considerably the nature of schools and their relationships with the outside world. Parents were given more rights and responsibilities, including the opportunity to serve on the governing body of their child's school. The 1988 Education Reform Act in particular, by introducing for the first time a National Curriculum, the testing of children at the ages of 7, 11, 14 and 16, and local management, including financial responsibility and the creation of new types of schools, was a radical break with the past. Furthermore, the disappearance of millions of jobs, along with other changes in our society, led to reforms not only of schools but also of further and higher education.

In the wake of such rapid and substantial changes it was not just parents and lay people, but also teachers and other professionals working in education, who found themselves struggling to keep up with what these many changes meant and how to get the best out of them. The *Education Matters* series addresses directly the major topics of reform, such as the new curriculum, testing and assessment, the role of parents and the handling of school finances, considering their effects on primary, secondary, further and higher education, and also the continuing education of adults.

The aim of the series is to present information about the challenges facing education in the remainder of the twentieth century in an authoritative but readable form. The books in the series, therefore, are of particular interest to parents, governors and all those concerned with education, but are written in such a way as to give an overview to students, experienced teachers and other professionals who work in the field.

Each book gives an account of the relevant legislation and

background, but, more importantly, stresses practical implications of change with specific examples of what is being or can be done to make reforms work effectively. The authors are not only authorities in their field, but also have direct experience of the matters they write about. That is why the *Education Matters* series makes an important contribution to both debate and practice.

ACKNOWLEDGEMENTS

I am indebted to Shirley Bull, Chris Reeve, Martin Powell and particularly Ted Raybould for the considerable impact they have had on my thinking about special education. Special thanks, as always, to Sue for her continued support and incisive comments on earlier drafts. Finally, thanks also to Anna and Jack, who continually lead me to re-evaluate my understanding of children's learning.

INTRODUCTION

This book introduces readers to current issues, concepts and practice in special education and focuses on factors teachers *can* influence in the classroom. It:

- sets developments in special education within a social and political context;
- relates classroom interactions to the wider contexts in which children learn and behave;
- emphasizes the importance of values and beliefs in influencing educational practice;
- provides a rationale for meeting children's 'special educational needs';
- presents an optimistic view of overcoming difficulties which highlights children's achievements.

The Education Acts of 1981 (Special Educational Needs) and 1988 have set a new agenda for special education. Changes are happening rapidly, particularly in relation to the curriculum, assessment and funding arrangements for children with special needs. In addition, further legislation is planned for the future which will have a significant impact on special education. However, irrespective of legislative changes and educational trends, many issues and principles remain constant and are central to promoting children's learning. The book focuses on these enduring features of educational practice.

Although a detailed explanation, analysis or critique of the law on special education is not undertaken, all the major elements of the recent legislation are considered and their likely influence on schools outlined, as follows:

- 1981 Education Act: Chapters 1, 2, 4 and 6;
- Local Management of Schools: Chapter 1;
- National Curriculum: Chapters 3 and 4;

- standard assessment tasks: Chapter 4;
- statutory assessment: Chapter 4;
- teacher assessment: Chapter 4.

The book concentrates on special needs within the ordinary school. Nevertheless, the principles identified apply equally to children and teachers in special schools. Similarly, different disabilities or impairments are not examined, in the belief that the principles of good teaching are generally applicable and transcend such categorization.

A recurring theme in the book is the way that values and beliefs influence classroom practice. They create our expectations for what children might achieve and subsequently influence our understanding of the teaching, learning and assessment process. Ultimately it will be the values and beliefs of those working with children, as well as their teaching skills, that determine whether or not difficulties are overcome and children's educational needs met.

Chapter 1

WHO HAS SPECIAL EDUCATIONAL NEEDS?

Introduction

This chapter examines the question 'Which children have special educational needs?'. In so doing it presents three perspectives on special education – historical, psychological and sociological – and assesses their impact on our understanding of how children learn and of their difficulties. The chapter concludes by highlighting major themes in special education which provide a framework for determining which children might have special educational needs.

When you think about children with special needs, which children immediately spring to mind? What kinds of problem do they experience? Are they children with behaviour problems or learning difficulties, or are they blind, deaf, physically impaired or mentally handicapped? For many people, images of handicapped children occur – children who depend on others for their welfare and are unlikely to lead independent lives.

Concepts of special education are undergoing a radical change, with the conventional wisdoms informing practice being challenged and reviewed. In any analysis of current events, we need to consider why certain children might be seen to have difficulties and to ask what shapes our own attitudes, values and perceptions towards special education and children with special educational needs.

We may have been influenced as pupils by our teachers' interactions with children presenting behaviour problems or having difficulties in learning. We are, however, as likely to be affected by what was absent from our educational environment as by our everyday experiences. In the main, we have been educated separately from peers who were blind, deaf or confined to wheelchairs. Children with recognized sensory, physical and mental handicaps have been filtered out of the mainstream system and taught separately in an alternative environment. Segregating children in this way conveys subtle messages to the children, families and communities of those who are removed, as well as those who remain within the mainstream sector.

Identifying which children require special education is not only a question of observing children over time and finding that they have particular attributes which make it unlikely that they will benefit from the ordinary school environment. It also depends on the attitudes and values we bring to bear when viewing all children, not only those potentially perceived to be experiencing difficulties. Seeing that a child in a wheelchair requires a special school rather than mainstream placement is as much a reflection of our beliefs as an indication of the child's needs.

One way of answering the question 'Who has special educational needs?' involves looking at the various perspectives that have dominated debates in the area of special education and the values and beliefs which underpin them. Examining these perspectives enables us to identify a number of trends which have emerged within the field of special education. The relevant perspectives are those of history, psychology and sociology.

Historical perspectives on special education

The first provision for those experiencing difficulties was created by charitable initiatives in the latter part of the eighteenth century. The first school for the deaf was established in the 1760s and the first for the blind in 1791. Provision for those with mental handicaps first appeared in 1847 and for those with physical handicaps it became available in 1865. Many of the early forms of special education were thus available to those with sensory deficits and mental deficiency. Children identified as requiring special provision tended to receive training rather than an education, the aim being to give them access to employment and to enable them to become productive members of society.

The Education Act of 1870 saw the extension of elementary education, and school boards set up special classes, initially for those with physical and sensory handicaps. Legislation towards the end of the nineteenth century endorsed the view that education should be compulsory for those with sensory handicaps. However, it was not until the early part of the next century that Acts of Parliament made it a mandatory requirement for school boards to make provision for those with physical handicaps.

Early forms of special provision were, therefore, targeted on those with physical, sensory and mental handicaps, which later extended to those children seen to have behavioural and emotional problems. The provision was made through voluntary organizations rather than by school boards or central government. These children were trained in specific skills and so became a relatively cheap form of labour. School boards and central government might have been expected to underpin their provision with alternative, less financially motivated aims.

Two further significant influences have shaped the development of special education. The first was the 'payment by results' scheme which operated in the early stages of formal state education. Under this scheme, teachers' salaries were linked to the educational achievements of their children. Inevitably those children performing poorly could be seen to jeopardize an otherwise healthy wage packet. One response to this potential dilemma was for teachers to suggest that anyone failing did so as a result of having a difficulty in learning which required other forms of educational provision. Teacher opinion provided the basis for recommending that children required a school placement outside the mainstream setting. Lack of progress was due to difficulties which only emerged in response to the teaching they received, rather than sensory, physical or mental handicaps.

The second influence on the development of special education concerned the emergence of intelligence testing as a major 'educational' instrument aimed at ascertaining children's learning potential. It also legitimized the view that poor progress was attributable to the personal characteristics of the child. Intelligence testing was developed in France and America in the early part of the twentieth century. Its use in the United Kingdom was promoted by Cyril Burt, the country's first educational psychologist. As we shall discuss in more detail in Chapter 2, Burt used intelligence tests to identify which children should be withdrawn from mainstream education to be placed in special schools. It was argued by advocates of intelligence testing that children with an IQ of less than 70 would make less satisfactory progress within the mainstream sector than their peers and would, therefore, benefit from the type of provision typically found in special schools.

The educational and political climate in the early part of the twentieth century facilitated these developments in promoting and legitimizing segregated forms of education. The focus on individual differences between children and the desire to establish pupils' learning potential had a major impact on educational provision, especially in terms of the practice of special education. The fact that the earliest forms of special provision were for those with physical and sensory difficulties, which were seen to be clearly identifiable medical conditions, gave the medical model (that is, that difficulties arise due to the characteristics of the child and that there is therefore something wrong with that child) considerable currency in special education.

The 1944 Education Act offered more formal recognition to intelligence testing and differential forms of education. Intelligence testing became an integral part of the Act through the introduction of the 11-plus. It was administered to predict which children would benefit from different forms of secondary education. Those who performed well were offered highly prized places in the academically prestigious grammar schools, while those failing received a more vocationally oriented curriculum in secondary modern and technical schools. The alleged predictive capacity of the intelligence test was also used to establish which children would benefit from special education. The Act described those with difficulties as having 'disabilities of body or mind' and so suggested again that problems arose because there was something wrong with the child.

The 1944 Education Act led to an increase in the number of recognized categories of special education from four to eleven. These new categories included the terms educationally subnormal–mild (ESN-M) and educationally subnormal–severe (ESN-S), thus distinguishing between different types of subnormality. The Act also introduced the term 'maladjustment' to refer to children presenting behavioural and emotional problems.

During the 1950s and 1960s, special education was still seen to be something that took place outside the mainstream. A large number of schools were built to cater for the increased demand in special provision required as a result of the new categories. By the 1960s the ESN-M population was by far the largest category of children ascertained as handicapped (64 per cent). The problems associated with attempting to predict future achievement using the 11-plus were emphasized by the introduction of comprehensive education. However, the arguments did not substantially influence the selection of children for placement in special schools. Educational psychologists steadily increased in number and continued to use intelligence tests on a widespread basis as the major form of assessing children's learning.

It was not until the mid- to late 1970s that increasing concern was expressed about the validity of offering differential provision for those seen to be experiencing difficulties. Arguments were advanced from a number of perspectives. First of all educational psychologists, as well as many others within the field of educational assessment, questioned the use of intelligence testing in special education. In particular, criticisms focused on their cultural bias and whether a child's performance reflected previous educational opportunities rather than learning potential.

Questions about the reliability of predicting future achievement were fuelled in part by research emerging from the United States, which suggested that when high-quality teaching was provided, children seen to be educationally disadvantaged could make excellent progress, commensurate with that of their peers. The score obtained on an IQ test was viewed as less important than the educational provision made available to help children learn.

Educationalists concerned about creating equal educational opportunities for children also questioned the provision of segregated special education. Segregation was not seen to be entirely compatible with the aims of offering all children equal educational opportunities irrespective of their gender, race, social class or perceived level of ability. Increasingly the call was made to integrate those with difficulties with their peers in the ordinary school.

The 1970s ended with the Warnock Report, which had been commissioned in 1974. The report can be seen as representing the state of thinking about special education at the time it was published, and it effectively shaped attitudes and practice for the 1980s. The report:

- suggested that the aims of education for children with special needs be the same for all children;
- recommended replacing notions of handicap with that of children's special needs;
- promoted the concept of integration;
- saw assessment as a gradual process taking place over time.

Some of the Warnock philosophy emerged in the 1981 Act on Special Needs, which came into force in April 1983.

In the years since the introduction of the 1981 Education Act, research has failed to indicate the extent to which the principles underpinning the Warnock Report have been implemented within LEAs. What does seem to have emerged with some consistency is the view that special educational provision differs markedly from one LEA to the next, and from one school to the next. The 1981 Education Act had significant resource implications for central government if successful implementation was to be secured. Those working within the field of special education, as in many other areas of education, also insist that adequate funds and resources were never forthcoming to meet the demands created by the legislation.

The 1988 Education Reform Act marks another watershed in the history of special education. While the practice it inspires might lead to further segregation of children found to be difficult to teach, in principle at least schools are urged to recognize that all children should have access to a similar curriculum. However, there are considerable concerns about the implications of the 1988 Act for children with special needs, particularly in relation to the new funding and assessment arrangements.

Perhaps one of the most significant effects of the new legislation is on the morale of the teaching profession. While the majority of teachers aim to overcome obstacles associated with a lack of funding and resources, current demands on teachers may mean that there is insufficient time or energy to ensure that children with difficulties are having their needs met.

Developments in special education do not occur in a vacuum. The prevailing political and economic climate in the country influences how children seen to have difficulties are to have their needs identified and met. It may be that a new educational orthodoxy emerges in the 1990s, driven by concerns about low standards and the effectiveness of 'modern teaching methods'. Teachers will have to be mindful of the past and its impact on special education if they are to resist the rhetoric of those on the next educational bandwagon.

Psychological perspectives on special education

Psychological perspectives on special education have emerged in part from their applications within the mainstream sector. Two perspectives can be seen to have had an influence on mainstream practice and are reflected in what have become known as child-centred and teacher-directed models of education.

Child-centred education

Current perceptions of child-centred education are heavily influenced by the developmental theories of Jean Piaget, the Swiss biologist and psychologist. His theories have led to views of children's learning and intellectual development which typically emphasize that 'how' children learn is more important that 'what' they learn; that the 'process' of learning is more significant than the outcomes or 'products' of learning.

Before Piaget, a number of theorists influenced child-centred education. Well-known educators such as Rousseau, Froebel and Montessori emphasized that the role of education is to facilitate children's development. They suggested that there were key stages during a child's life when different aspects of development could best be encouraged. Froebel referred to these occasions as 'budding points', whereas Montessori preferred the term 'sensitive periods'. Developmental theory has influenced perceptions of the curriculum and child-centred education but currently exerts a less dominant presence. For some, a curriculum based on developmental theory is seen virtually to deny any directive role to education.

A subsequent influence on child-centred education was those stressing the central role of direct experience on children's learning. These theorists share some ground with developmental thinkers, since developmentalists recognize that certain experiences are more likely to promote development than others. However, experiential theorists such as Dewey envisaged a learning process which was continually evolving not in some predetermined manner (as implied by theorists of development) but in one dependent upon the meaning that children had derived from previous experience. The teacher acts as a facilitator, creating stimulating learning environments, within which children can explore and learn for themselves.

Piaget provides a bridge between developmental and experiential theories. His views of intellectual development have provided the inspiration for much child-centred educational practice. Piaget believed that children passed through distinct stages of intellectual development, and that children's learning was facilitated through their experiences and interactions with their environment. It is fundamental to this approach that the learner should be at the heart of any attempt to appreciate the nature of the curriculum. Knowledge cannot be prescribed with any certainty and is acquired through experience. It is seen to be tentative and, rather than being distinct from the learner, cannot be separated from the sense that individuals derive from their experience and discoveries. It is argued that since each child construes its own understanding of the world, planning learning for children cannot take any other form than arranging appropriate learning experiences in which children's development can flourish. The classroom is then geared to stimulate children, to encourage interest and for their learning to be based on their own experiences. The teacher is a facilitator, promoting learning and acting as the child's guide in the learning process. Investigative learning is at the heart of the approach to teaching.

The child-centred philosophy, with its focus on the development of individual children, can be seen to be closely associated with a specific cause of children's difficulties. The primary reason for failure is often attributed to 'within-child' factors. Children fail to make progress because there is something wrong with them. Problems are frequently attributed to the child's level of intellectual development not being commensurate with that of peers. A failure to learn was closely associated, therefore, with faulty intellectual development. A failure to behave acceptably was attributed to a child's slow rate of social and emotional development.

Child-centred education can also be seen to have been compatible with a form of assessment which stressed the failings of children and attempted to identify what aspect of their cognitive or social functioning was awry and needed remedying. Typically, this form of assessment relied on the administration of a range of tests of cognitive ability and academic progress. These usually included tests of intelligence, reading and mathematics. Success or failure on each test was determined through comparisons with children of comparable age and social background on whom each test was piloted.

Child-centred education has been the dominant philosophy within the primary sector in recent times. It was promoted in the Plowden Report and is widely encouraged in many textbooks for teachers. None the less, the early 1990s have seen a widespread attack on child-centred education from politicians, teachers and academics. Reports of falling standards and the almost impossibly high demands the theory places on teachers have fuelled arguments for a return to more formal class teaching, less topic work and more subject specialism. However, research into primary education suggests that child-centred education was never adopted on the scale imagined by its critics.

What also needs to be recognized is that it has a number of appealing features. These include:

- children becoming active participants in the learning process;
- a recognition that teaching has to be tailored to the needs of individual children;
- an appreciation that the curriculum must be developed to cater for children of different attainments;
- a move towards less formal teaching arrangements.

Some of the limitations of child-centred education could be seen as:

- the implications when children fail;
- the difficulties of successfully implementing the philosophy in the classroom;
- the problems of letting children develop at their own rate.

Teacher-directed education

It is more difficult to define teacher-directed education than child-centred education, as it encompasses two contradictory interpretations. In the first interpretation, teacher-directed education is closely associated with traditional teaching approaches which aim to impart specific subject matter through methods that emphasize memory and rote learning, and in which the pupils are largely passive. Teachers disseminate skills, knowledge and information which represent the beliefs, attitudes and values of the dominant culture in society. It is the 'filling of empty vessels' concept, and difficulties are seen to arise from a child's inability to learn effectively. This approach represents the thinking behind the elementary schools of the past and remains central to a number of educators and commentators on education today. This traditional view of teacher-directed education has been welcomed by those on the political right and was advocated by the authors of the 'Black Papers' in the late 1960s and early 1970s. They challenged the rise of progressivism, which they perceived to be embodied in models of child-centred education.

The appeal of this interpretation lies in the belief that:

- it is easier to organize teaching on the basis of a class than of a group or individuals;
- it leads to higher standards, particularly in literacy and numeracy;
- teaching is more effective when children are grouped according to their abilities.

While an undeniable case can be made for whole-class teaching at times, the assumption that this will be any more effective in meeting individual needs, even where children are grouped according to their abilities, must be questioned. It is difficult to anticipate how the same lesson content can satisfy the learning requirements of 30 or more children. In addition, there is no reason to believe that the skills involved in whole-class teaching are more readily learned than, or even at times significantly different from, those necessary for organizing learning in a more formal manner. Effective teaching requires teachers to have considerable knowledge and skills in a number of areas (for example, knowledge of the curriculum, identifying and diagnosing errors, questioning, assessment, etc.), irrespective of the organizational arrangements for grouping or seating children.

An alternative view of teacher-directed education aims to develop a theory of teaching. Its proponents argue that it is impossible to develop general principles of teaching if children are unique and so require their own specifically designed teaching programme. Principles of teaching will only emerge through looking at what children have in common. It is argued that the child-centred philosophy would lead to more effective practice if underpinned by a theory of teaching. The focus is on what teachers do that leads to successful learning. The aim is to look at the teaching and learning environment in order to pinpoint similarities in practice which promote children's learning. In effect this means examining what children are taught, how they are taught and patterns of classroom organization, as well as the skills and attributes children bring to the learning environment. The proponents of this view of teacher-directed education have distanced themselves from the alternative interpretation advanced in the 'Black Papers' and by those who argue for more traditional teaching methods.

This interpretation of teacher-directed education pins a failure to learn on aspects of the learning environment and the educational provision that children receive, rather than on the children themselves. Initial attempts to resolve difficulties through looking at the learning environment were narrow in scope and tended to restrict assessment to the curriculum and the nature of the tasks children received. It was argued that by adapting and amending the curriculum, children's difficulties in learning could be overcome. A more sophisticated investigation of the learning environment incorporated an assessment of not only the curriculum but also:

- patterns of classroom organization;
- the nature and range of activities on which children become engaged;
- the ways tasks and activities are presented to children;
- children's relationship with peers;
- the meaning, value and sense children attach to their learning activities.

In other words, any aspect of the classroom or school which influences children's learning may be the cause of their difficulties.

The appeal of this interpretation of teacher-directed education can be seen to lie in:

- the recognition that it is the teacher's responsibility to help children overcome problems;
- the focus on the learning environment and not the child as a potential source of difficulties;
- the fact that it is non-labelling and optimistic, as it appreciates both that children can learn when offered appropriate learning experiences, and that there are clear teaching strategies which have been successful in enabling children with difficulties to learn effectively.

The limitations of some forms of teacher-directed education can be summarized as:

- a tendency for pupils to remain passive in the learning process;
- a tendency towards more formal teaching approaches;
- an excessive emphasis on basic skills and not enough attention paid to whether children can generalize and apply their knowledge.

Typically, the debates over child-centred and teacher-directed education reinforce existing prejudices and polarize views. This tends to pre-empt any attempt to examine either approach dispassionately or to explore their potentially complementary roles in the classroom. So, for example, discussion might focus on the respective merits of whole-class versus group teaching, rather than considering the circumstances under which one may be more appropriate than the other. These issues are considered further in Chapter 3.

Psychological applications in education have changed markedly in recent years. This can be attributed in part to the influence of sociological perspectives on special education, which will now be examined.

Sociological perspectives on special education

Sociological perspectives on special education have attempted to place the progress that individual children make in a social context. Sociologists argue that children's learning is influenced by many factors in addition to the quality of teaching they receive. Children's learning outcomes can thus be seen to be related to their social class, their race and their gender. In addition, the personal attributes of teachers cannot be ignored in gaining an understanding of the factors influencing learning.

Initially sociological perspectives looked at the handicapped or those deemed to have considerable difficulties, and investigated how they fitted into society at large. What was their impact on family life or on the community? Early perspectives accepted the notion of there being children with difficulties who were different from their peers, and implied a shared understanding of what was normal and what was not normal. Individuals were seen to perform certain functions in society which helped maintain the generally smooth running of that society. For some, special education was a way of controlling others.

This sociological perspective gave way to an alternative philosophy which stressed the tensions and conflicts between different groups in society. An understanding of economic, political and social circumstances was seen to be crucial to appreciating developments taking place in special education. The social construction and maintenance of special education and the involvement of its participants were also areas of concern.

Sociologists have raised a number of crucial questions about the nature of special education. For example, they have asked whose interests are being served by placing certain sections of the school population outside the mainstream sector, and they have been instrumental in identifying the fact that certain social and racial groups are over-represented in samples of children receiving forms of special education.

Sociological perspectives have also heightened our awareness of the vested interests of professional groups in the field of special education. Initially special education was administered by medical officers and was seen to be a medical condition. In 1974, children with difficulties became the responsibility of local education authorities. Instead of medical officers making placement decisions about children's education, the reponsibility fell to those employed by education authorities, with educational psychologists playing a particularly influential role. This served to create tension between medical officers and educational psychologists and reflected anxieties surrounding the shifting balance of power between the two professional groups.

It was reasonable to ask who would benefit from these and other changes. Could the actions of individuals representing different professional groups be viewed as solely in the interest of the pupils concerned, or were they at times acting to assert their own position and indispensability?

The law and special educational needs

So far the discussion has traced developments in special education and the way children with difficulties have been viewed. In answering the question 'Who has special educational needs?', the definition enshrined in the 1981 Education Act offers a legal interpretation which needs to be considered. However, this may be revised in the future.

Whereas previous legislation has defined difficulties in terms of the characteristics of individual children, the 1981 Act defines special needs in terms of the *educational provision* required to meet a child's needs, as follows: 'A child has special educational needs if he has a learning difficulty which calls for special provision to be made for him.' Special educational needs are thus defined in terms of whether or not a child has a learning difficulty which requires special educational provision. It is the presence or absence of appropriate resources within a child's existing school environment which ultimately determines whether a child has special educational needs. It is not simply a matter of assessing the individual characteristics of a child in isolation without reference to the contexts

15

in which learning takes place. A child cannot be assessed without reference to its current educational environment.

In the 1981 Act, it was anticipated that approximately 2 per cent of the school population would require LEAs to make special educational provision available to meet their educational needs. These children would have their needs assessed formally through the statutory assessment procedure (see Chapter 4), and have a *statement* issued which identified both their educational needs and the provision to be made available to meet them. They would frequently be placed in special schools, although LEAs were encouraged to meet their needs in the ordinary school where possible. However, the Act also stated that there was a much larger group of children, somewhere in the region of a further 18 per cent of the school population, who would have special needs which would be met within the mainstream system. The children concerned would not have a statement issued detailing their needs or provision to meet them.

The group comprising the 2 per cent will be the subject of a detailed multi-disciplinary assessment; the larger group (18 per cent) will not. The 1981 Act can therefore be seen to create and draw attention to two groups of children who have special educational needs. The legislation does not, however, provide guidance or detailed criteria for teachers, except in the most general terms, on how to establish which children fall into either category.

The link between special needs and available provision means there are considerable differences in the numbers of children requiring a statement in different LEAs. Two children with similar educational needs, but in neighbouring authorities, could receive different treatment under the Act. One might be assessed as having special educational needs because additional provision had to be made available to meet its needs. However, the other might be receiving the appropriate provision from the school's existing resources and so would not require additional 'special educational provision' to be made available.

Such discrepancies could also exist within an LEA, since

schools inevitably do not use their finances and resources in the same way. Schools differ in their priorities, philosophies and educational practice. The allocation of resources is a reflection of this, with the result that some schools are better equipped than others to meet the needs of the child experiencing problems, and so are less likely to initiate the statutory assessment procedure.

Inconsistencies in LEA practice generated by the definition of 'special educational needs' enshrined in the 1981 Education Act were noted by the Audit Commission and Her Majesty's Inspectorate (1992). They recommend that there should be national guide-lines defining the level of children's needs which require additional help from an LEA.

Determining which children have special needs is a matter with major financial implications. These have been highlighted through debates on Local Management of Schools (LMS). Increasingly, funds are being diverted towards schools and away from local authorities. LEAs still determine the rationale through which money is be distributed, but it is headteachers and teachers who decide how funds are to be deployed.

When allocating funds, LEAs can take into account the number of children with special needs (18 per cent) in ordinary schools, and the schools they attend. However, money cannot be targeted at specific children: it has to be included in the overall amount received by schools. It is then the responsibility of the school to ensure that children with difficulties have the necessary resources to meet their needs. The inevitable concern is that schools may not use funds for the children for whom they were intended. In an educational climate where resources are scarce, the temptation will be to put finances into areas which schools consider need more immediate attention. Equally, schools may not have adequate funds to make provision for the 18 per cent of children with special needs.

This situation could create tension between parents and schools. Aggrieved parents who feel their child's needs are not being met may approach the LEA, only to be informed that schools have been given the resources and that it is the schools' responsibility to ensure they are used to meet children's special educational needs. Teachers need to work closely with parents so that they appreciate the constraints that schools are currently working within.

As more money is now going directly to schools, less is being retained centrally by LEAs for special need support services, such as educational psychologists, specialist teaching staff or inspectors. These services face an uncertain future as the full implications of LMS are realized. It is quite possible that they will be severely cut in future years or that schools will receive money directly to buy in their services if and when they are required. This would severely limit the scope and potential of the preventive work which was a marked feature of many of these support services.

LEAs are still responsible for maintaining the educational provision for statemented children with special educational needs, whether they be in mainstream or special schools. LMS is scheduled to be introduced to all special schools in 1994. This may have advantages in some instances. However, the very nature of the difficulties experienced by some children who are brain-damaged or severely physically disabled defies the idea that resourcing their needs can be accomplished by an authority-wide formula. Nowhere are the uncertainties of special education clearer than in relation to LMS.

From the discussion so far, a number of themes emerge which are central to an appreciation of the development of special education and to an understanding of which children are seen to have special educational needs.

Identification and assessment

Some changes have occurred in the way children with difficulties are identified. This topic is discussed in detail in Chapter 3. However, it is helpful to bear in mind that at one time, if children failed to progress at a comparable rate to peers, it was inevitably assumed that there was something wrong with the child. The usual explanation given was the child's low intellectual capacity, which resulted in an inability to learn effectively.

Increasingly concerns have been expressed about such a singular focus, and this has led to other factors being acknowledged as influential in promoting children's learning. The focus of assessment has thus been expanded to take account of the broader environment in which learning takes place. There is still a recognition that what children bring to the learning environment is also significant: nevertheless, the relevance of the curriculum, children's motivation to learn and previous learning experiences are more important than estimates of intelligence and trying to ascertain potential achievements.

These developments have taken place in relation to assessing children's learning and behaviour difficulties, areas where ambiguity exists over who actually has a problem. For other children, whose difficulties have a physical basis, the notion that it is the child's problem is less readily refuted. While we might argue about the circumstance leading to a child's troublesome classroom behaviour and suggest that incidents of disruption would decrease if there were changes in the classroom environment, could we make the same case for children with impaired vision or hearing, or who are in wheelchairs? Our typical understanding of their circumstances may lead us to think that they have the problem. We can see immediately how their lives differ from our own and recognize that whatever the curriculum or quality of teaching, those pupils are still going to be blind, deaf or physically impaired.

While this is undoubtedly the case, it is dangerous to infer that these are homogeneous groups of children who inevitably experience problems. It is now recognized that children adapt and respond in a variety of ways to potentially handicapping conditions, and that the curriculum and teaching approaches are just as important in determining learning outcomes as for any children thought to have difficulties.

This leads to a second theme in special education – integration.

Integration

Integration is the process of teaching children with special educational needs within mainstream settings. It can take many forms and was given increased prominence following the publication of the Warnock Report in 1978 and the 1981 Education Act. As stated earlier in the chapter, early forms of special education provided for children with difficulties outside the mainstream setting. The assumptions underpinning special education were challenged during the 1970s and the growth of segregated special education, which had proceeded unabated in the 1950s and 1960s, can be seen to have peaked. Increasingly educationalists questioned the basis on which children were being excluded from mainstream education, and initiatives to integrate children with difficulties into the ordinary school were mounted. In the case of children seen to have moderate learning difficulties and behaviour problems, steps were taken to adopt intervention strategies within the mainstream school so that future placement in a special school would not be necessary. At the same time, it was hoped that children already in special schools would receive some part of their education within the ordinary school environment wherever possible.

The Warnock Report supported the case for integrating children with special needs into ordinary schools, and the 1981 Education Act also tacitly endorsed this policy. However, to integrate effectively requires appropriate funding and resources, which were not forthcoming when the Act was implemented. As a result, the optimism generated in relation to integration in the late 1970s and early 1980s was short-lived, as the economic realities effectively scuppered attempts to promote the genuine integration of children with special educational needs.

Parental involvement

In keeping with the general political climate of the 1980s, where central government sought to give increased power to parents, the political rhetoric and subsequent legislation within the field of special education gave parents an increased voice in their children's education. Parents became more involved in the assessment of children's educational needs and were urged to take a full part in the decision-making process about their children's future education. While there is an undeniable case for parents being full and active partners with teachers and administrators in their children's education, the problem arises when, for one reason or another, some parents are not in a position to take full advantage of the rights they appear to have been given. This will be considered in more detail in Chapter 6.

Parental involvement within their children's education has also been sought in two further ways. First, the 1980 Education Act gave parents increased representation on governing bodies. This legislation together with the 1988 Education Act significantly changed the role and status of governing bodies. Parents were encouraged to express their rights through this channel. Governors have extensive responsibilities which include making appropriate provision for children with special needs.

Second, during the 1970s and 1980s, professionals within the special education sector were inviting parents to help teach their children important educational skills at home, in partnership with teachers in school. Many mainstream schools developed reading projects which asked parents to participate in helping their children learn how to read. The parents of pre-school handicapped children frequently became involved in Portage projects (see Chapter 6) or similar LEA-developed initiatives.

The responsibility of the school

Initially, the role of the school was to inform the necessary personnel that children were experiencing difficulties which required a special school placement. Schools played little part in the subsequent assessment and decision-making process about how best to meet children's needs. The 1981 and 1988 Education Acts gave schools considerably greater responsibility in identifying, assessing and making recommendations about provision for children with special educational needs.

21

It is now the responsibility of governors to ensure that the National Curriculum is implemented, and to satisfy parents that appropriate provision is available to meet the educational needs of children with difficulties. Teachers now play a central role in the identification and assessment process and have parity with other professionals in this respect.

The impact of all these developments on children with special needs is, at the time of writing, not entirely clear. Inevitably the Key Stage assessments and the duty to report results are causing anxieties. Schools will of course wish to be seen as effective and may be concerned that parental perceptions of their efficacy will be moderated by the presence of children with special needs. These children are often seen as requiring more valuable time and resources at the expense of their peers. The question to be faced by schools is whether the extra demands that children with special needs make can be met within the new scenario.

This chapter has outlined three perspectives which have contributed to an understanding of which children have special educational needs. It has also considered the legal definition of 'special educational needs' and highlighted some of the problems this has created. The chapter has concluded with an overview of recent developments in special education. Chapter 2 takes a more critical look at the concept of special education, and asks whether or not it may be discriminatory and mean that large numbers of children are not having their educational needs met.

Chapter 2

SPECIAL NEEDS: A DISCRIMINATORY CONCEPT?

Introduction

Increasingly teachers are being urged to recognize that schools that successfully meet the demands of a diverse range of individual needs are also invariably effective in meeting special educational needs. Effective teaching is effective special education. In Chapter 1, the background to and trends in special education were discussed. The nature of recent developments could enable those in the field of special education to make a significant contribution to the ways in which all children are taught, not only those presenting problems. Mainstream teachers are currently addressing many issues, particularly in relation to assessment, that are familiar to their colleagues working in special education. Whether or not the envisaged contribution is made depends on the willingness of teachers to challenge educational myths about children, teaching and learning that underpin much current thinking and practice in special education.

This chapter questions assumptions about the concept of 'special educational needs' on which existing practice is based, and in doing so explores the following themes:

- educational myths which impinge on our thinking about children's learning;
- language usage in special education and its role in promulgating educational myths;
- values underpinning practice in special education.

Myths in special education

The word 'myth' is usually applied to a story or account of the world that has grown up without necessarily being supported by evidence. In this way, its use is not unlike the meaning conveyed by the term 'conventional wisdom'. In everyday language, myths have a grain of truth in them, but in all probability are seen to be difficult to substantiate and unlikely to be upheld following close critical scrutiny. Myths take on a meaning that outweighs their origins.

For social anthropologists, the term 'myth' has a technical meaning which refers to the process whereby stories or accounts of the world grow up within a culture. What is therefore important about myths is not that they are wrong or out of all proportion to their origin, but that they are active and become mechanisms of control within the culture. The power of myths in education generally, and special education specifically, is that they can control the way people think and behave. Myths pre-empt debate and can lead us into ways of seeing the world that shape our behaviour. Within the field of education, we become receptive to arguments and practice that we might otherwise reject. By their very nature, we rarely examine the source of myths or their impact on practice.

There are a number of myths pervading special education; for example, that the number of children experiencing difficulties at some time during their school careers may be as many as one in five, that children with difficulties need one-to-one tuition, that they cannot concentrate for long periods, etc. These commonly held views set the agenda for how we think about children, how they learn, how they can be taught and where they should be taught.

The myth of one in five

Following the publication of the Warnock Report (DES, 1978), perhaps the most frequently quoted myth in special education is the belief that up to one in five children might have a difficulty in learning at some time during their school careers. The impact of this myth sustains teacher expectations for children failing to learn on a basis that might be wholly unjustified. The issue to be addressed here is the way evidence has been used to create the myth. It is likely that, rather than enabling children to receive the appropriate provision to meet their needs, this belief sets the agenda for widespread discrimination on a scale that is rarely acknowledged.

References to the 'Warnock 20 per cent' are now commonplace in books, articles and the press, and several recent publications have made direct reference to this in their titles, such as *One in Five: the assessment and incidence of special educational needs* (Croll and Moses, 1985). In their book *Warnock's Eighteen Per Cent: children with special needs in the primary school*, Gipps, Gross and Goldstein (1987) referred to those children who Warnock thought had special needs but would continue to be educated in the mainstream school. The other 2 per cent would be taught in special schools.

The Warnock Committee wished to estimate the incidence of special needs and reached their conclusion after examining evidence drawn from four sources. On the basis of their review of the evidence, the Warnock Report declared that:

> the planning of services for children and young people should be based on the assumption that about one in six children at any time, and up to one in five children at some time during their school career, will require some form of special educational provision. (p. 41)

However, the evidence on which these estimates are based relies on a number of features including the use of IQ data to identify children experiencing difficulties. Although it can be concluded, as the committee did, that up to one in five children may have difficulties, other interpretations are just as legitimate.

Another equally valid conclusion which could be drawn from examining the evidence available to the Warnock Committee is that in any class, irrespective of the number of children being taught or their attainments, teachers will have difficulties meeting the educational needs of all the children. What we might be dealing with is a problem of teacher management, rather than one concerned with the learning characteristics of children. Thus, the figure of one in five reflects the proportion of children in any classroom, in any type of school, that teachers experience difficulties in teaching.

At the time the Warnock Committee reported, the prevailing thinking, as discussed in Chapter 1, was that there was a clearly identifiable group of children who would at some time during their school careers experience a difficulty in learning. Concern was expressed at the continued use of categories of handicap to define and describe difficulties, and the Warnock Committee instead introduced the notion of special educational needs. The committee did not, however, challenge the more substantive issues of the aetiology of difficulties. Similarly, it did not make much reference to the view that children's failure to learn has to be considered in relation to their learning experiences and learning environment. As a result, the committee did not debate the inherent dangers of predicting the proportion of the school population that might experience difficulties, or query the evidence on which these percentages were based.

Estimates of the incidence of special needs were based, in part, on children's performances on IQ tests. When the committee reported, the widespread use of intelligence testing was an accepted form of assessing children's progress and establishing whether or not they might have a difficulty in learning. Since that time, the role of psychometric assessment has been challenged on methodological and moral grounds.

The IQ of 70 which was adopted in the studies quoted in Warnock has been recognized by many educators as the cut-off point for determining whether children have difficulties which warrant a placement in a special school. However, we often forget where that figure comes from. It is derived from the work of Cyril Burt, the first educational psychologist to be appointed in the country. Burt wished to employ an objective measure for determining placement in the available special schools. The London County Council had places for approximately 1.5 per cent of the school population. Burt found that this figure could be met by using an IQ of 69.4 as the cut-off point. The figure of 70 which is firmly fixed in people's minds as a convenient criterion for selection for special education, and which has had such a widespread influence on the lives of many children, was originally adopted on purely pragmatic grounds to fill the number of available places in London schools.

There is no discussion in the Warnock Report about the concern, or even controversy, regarding the criteria adopted in the studies for investigating the incidence of special educational needs. It is ironic that Warnock promotes a move away from categories of handicap and towards integration, yet uses data to estimate incidence of difficulties that are based on the 'old ways of thinking' which have so successfully oiled the wheels of segregated education.

Recent developments in special education and assessment are leading to an increased focus on the interactive nature of learning, and on the fact that an examination of what children learn cannot be divorced from considerations of how they are taught and the contexts in which learning takes place. These developments are reviewed and discussed in Chapter 3.

The implications of believing that one in five children are going to experience difficulties are very different from thinking that, in any class, teachers will feel that approximately 20 per cent of children are not receiving the appropriate tuition. The former leads us to look at the learning characteristics of children; the latter leads us to an assessment of the learning environment, the quality of teaching and the appropriateness of existing provision. Believing that up to one in five children may experience difficulties can be seen as legitimizing children's failure to learn. However, if teachers acknowledged that the 'one in five' is based on dubious evidence which needs to be carefully examined, they would be bringing a very different perspective to bear on educational practice.

The myth that children with special needs have learning difficulties or behaviour problems

Chapters 3 and 5 respectively explore in detail the myths that some children have a difficulty in learning or experience behaviour problems, and examine the complex nature of classroom interactions. It is argued that children's learning and behaviour do not exist in a vacuum and should therefore be considered in relation to the various factors which influence their development.

The myth that children with special educational needs require one-to-one tuition

An inevitable concern of teachers when planning to teach children seen to have difficulties is the amount of time available each day to give them the attention it is felt they need. How valid is such a concern?

A common assumption about children with special needs is that they need to be placed in smaller-sized teaching groups or, in an ideal world, receive one-to-one tuition. Even if the resources were available, would it be desirable to teach children on a one-to-one basis? Inevitably it is also assumed that those children presenting problems in the mainstream classroom will demand more of our time. Equally, we are led to believe that if there were fewer children in the class such problems would be dealt with more satisfactorily.

Yet what kind of learning environment would children experience if they were being taught solely on a one-to-one basis? There would be no opportunities for them to work cooperatively with peers. Recent research suggests that children seen to experience difficulties derive considerable benefits from working collaboratively alongside their peers. Through working in partnership, children learn many important social skills that are essential for later life.

Children also require opportunities to work on their own when they are practising newly acquired skills so that their initial learning is consolidated. Similarly, if children are to be given an opportunity to solve problems and apply skills, knowledge and concepts, some of this must take place through their working on their own or with peers, away from the immediate supervision of the teacher. At such times the teacher does not provide any direct input but offers children an opportunity to work things out for themselves.

It is doubtful whether any productive work, specifically tailored to meet the needs of individual pupils, can ever be undertaken without appropriate preparation on the part of the teacher. It is helpful to make a distinction between the time set aside for *planning* and that available for actual *teaching*. Additional planning and preparation time may well be necessary for those children who present us with problems. This may be needed to adapt the curriculum so that it becomes more appropriate for the children with difficulties, or it might involve the preparation of additional teaching materials. This, however, is done outside the classroom, and while time still needs to be found, teaching need not be on a one-to-one basis. In other words, children with difficulties require no more of the teacher's direct time in the classroom than any other child.

So even if the resources were available it is highly questionable whether providing children with one-to-one attention would be advisable. The call for such pupil–teacher ratios could again be seen to reflect the not inconsiderable difficulties teachers face in meeting the individual needs of all the children in the class.

The myth that children with special educational needs cannot concentrate for long periods

Do children with special needs have greater difficulty in concentrating than anyone else? We know from our own personal experience that we achieve different levels of concentration for the areas of life that interest and motivate us. Ask us to read a book that is of only minimal interest and our capacity for making cups of tea or engaging in strenuous avoidance activities increases quite markedly. In contrast a book that we find stimulating dramatically increases our powers of concentration. It is likely that children will respond in similar ways when faced with tasks and activities that they either enjoy or dislike.

Research examining children's learning experiences in primary schools found that teachers could often ascertain when work they gave children was too difficult because pupils became distracted and did not concentrate on the task in hand. However, they *never* estimated that work was too easy, because children were able to show acceptable levels of concentration on tasks which were too easy. In other words the very same children who failed to concentrate when work was too difficult were nevertheless able to do so when the work was too easy. It is likely that the extent to which they can concentrate is closely associated to the work they are given. Where it is purposeful, meaningful and stimulating, children are more likely to be able to display suitable levels of concentration than when this is not the case.

These myths and others have taken a firm hold in our educational culture and it is almost irrelevant whether or not they can be supported if held up to careful examination. They set an agenda for how we think about children, how they learn, how they behave, how they can be taught and where they should be taught. Their purpose is to maintain patterns of educational practice that are resistant to change. The powerful influence myths exert is due in part to our willingness to believe them. They fit our view of the world.

Myths and language usage

How is it that these myths are so widely known and accepted? The next section examines the way these myths are promulgated through our use of language. There are aspects of language usage in special education which promote educational myths and may have discriminative overtones through the expectations created for children's learning. Three themes related to language usage will be explored:

- discriminatory language;
- the concept of 'ability';
- the label 'special educational needs'.

Discriminatory language

Education is about communicating, about influencing the development of people, about shaping the ideas and the behaviour of future generations. Education relies heavily on language, not only as an integral part of the teaching process, but also as a means of controlling the content, methods and values in that process. We hope our chosen language conveys to a listener our intended meaning. We may recognize, though, that this will depend in part on the previous experiences of the listeners and the interpretation they impose on what is heard.

Unfortunately, from time to time, we may also convey meanings of which we are unaware and which we do not intend. In recent years, those working in the field of education have become concerned to address discriminative elements in language, particularly in relation to racism and sexism, which convey undesired but powerful messages. Let me now illustrate how language usage enables discriminatory practice to be pinpointed:

- What would you think if I suggested that black children should sit separately in the classroom, should be withdrawn for their lessons from the mainstream classroom, and should be given different work from the rest of the class? You would probably think that I was *racist*.
- What would you think if I suggested that girls should sit separately in the classroom, should be withdrawn for their lessons from the mainstream classroom, and should be given different work from the boys? You would probably think that I was *sexist*.
- However, what would you say if I suggested that some children who were experiencing difficulties with their work should sit separately in the classroom, should be withdrawn for their lessons from the mainstream classroom, and should be given different work from the rest of the class? 'Good' special needs education has often adopted similar practices, but if you do not find it acceptable, how would you describe such discrimination?

Whereas we recognize discrimination based on race and gender, and have evolved a vocabulary to describe it ('racism' and 'sexism'), there is no word for discrimination based on handicap. As a result, it is harder to draw attention to and overcome. Although a positive interpretation is possible for withdrawing children from the mainstream classroom (so that they can receive additional help), would we condone such practice if the children being withdrawn were to be identified on the basis of their race or gender?

The above example serves to illustrate the lack of an appropriate vocabulary to articulate discrimination where we feel it occurs in special education. Furthermore, not only do we lack the means to focus attention on potentially discriminating circumstances, but reservations can be expressed about the seemingly acceptable, apparently non-discriminatory, widely used terms *special educational needs* and *integration*. The concept of special education needs can be seen as concealing institutionalized discrimination. Croll and Moses (1985), in their study on the incidence of special needs in ordinary schools, found that the ratio of boys to girls seen to experience special needs was almost two to one. In terms of areas of difficulty, the most dramatic differences were in relation to behaviour problems, where boys outnumbered girls by almost four to one. Croll and Moses also report, although cautiously, that more children from ethnic minority backgrounds are seen to have special needs than white children.

Turning to the concept of integration, arguments in favour of integrating children with special needs into ordinary schools are often predicated on the belief that these children differ from their peers, that they have special needs, but that they should nevertheless be taught in mainstream settings. There is rarely any acknowledgement that children with special needs are potentially being identified, in part, as a result of their race, gender or social class. A question that remains largely unanswered is the extent to which teacher perceptions, expectations and prejudices contribute to children being seen to have special educational needs.

It is possible that we discriminate against large numbers of children within the education system through the organizational arrangements we make to cater for their educational needs. However, these are rarely if ever challenged because we have not evolved the language to identify and articulate such discrimination. Our familiarity with the concepts of special educational needs and integration, and the positive connotations they often convey, make us less sensitive to the potentially discriminative practice and thinking they promote and endorse.

The concept of 'ability'

A second issue related to language usage and the transmission of myths concerns the way certain children may have learning opportunities denied them through teachers' descriptions of their academic performance. Think of the euphemisms for describing children with ability: 'bright', 'high flyer', 'quick', 'whizz kids', 'able', etc. These descriptions reflect perceptions of those children and, even more significantly, create expectations for future achievement through implying a general competence. It is often inferred that this is innate and a teacher might be led to believe that, because the children possess such ability, predictions can be made about future attainments.

The way educationalists refer to children's 'ability' is a potentially insidious form of discrimination. Although we may no longer support the use of intelligence tests to ascertain children's ability and learning potential, the language of the intelligence test still abounds. This may, in the most negative instances, lead to children being quite arbitrarily identified as lacking in intelligence or ability, with the inevitable consequence that expectations for their future learning are low.

The School Examinations and Assessment Council (SEAC, 1989) has published materials on assessment which provide advice to schools on how to implement classroom-based teacher assessment. Pack C of these materials is potentially quite radical in drawing attention to the way we use the word 'ability'. The guide says the following about the concept of ability: 'assessment in the context of the national curriculum has not been designed to predict how well a child will do in later life, by trying in some way to measure ability or effort' (p. 5); and 'assessment in the context of the national curriculum relates to achievement. It does not relate to attitude or personality' (p. 15). The emphasis in the materials is on what children have achieved and not on speculating what they might learn in the future, on the basis of hypothesized levels of ability.

The issue merits examination because language defining children's ability reflects fundamental assumptions and perceptions about the nature of children's learning, which are rarely challenged and critically examined. If we referred to gender or racial differences in a way which served to promote differential learning opportunities and outcomes, it would be challenged immediately, and rightly so. Similar concern should be expressed about descriptions of children in terms of their 'ability'.

The label 'special educational needs'

This lead me to the final theme related to language and myths, which concerns the use of the term 'special educational needs'. In special education, using labels has been accepted practice for a long time. Terms such as 'idiot', 'imbecile', 'defective', 'feeble-minded' and 'educationally subnormal' were once an accepted part of educational language and were enshrined in legislation, just as the term 'special needs' is at the moment.

There is now a general awareness of labelling theory and its damaging consequence. Nevertheless, what seems to be happening in special education is that we have become increasingly sophisticated in our use of labels. Could it be that children deemed 'idiots' through government legislation in 1913, who were then described as 'severely subnormal' in 1945 and became 'educationally subnormal' in 1962, are now known as 'children with special needs'?

The term 'special educational needs', as well as referring to those children who become the subject of statements, is a more general term for any child seen to be experiencing a difficulty. What should be remembered is that the legal epithet 'special needs' is defined not in terms of the characteristics of children but in relation to existing provision. There are two problems with the term which it is helpful to highlight:

- distinguishing between needs and provision;
- defining educational needs.

There is general ambiguity about the difference between needs and provision. The following statement appeared in *A Curriculum for All* (NCC, 1989b) about pupils' teaching needs:

> pupils with S.E.N. are likely to have even stronger needs than other pupils for:
>
> - positive attitudes from school staff,
> - partnerships with teachers,
> - a climate of warmth and support,
> - emphasis on profiles of achievement,
> - home–school partnerships. (p. 8)

In a section headed 'different forms of special educational needs' the Warnock Report stated the following:

> In very broad terms special educational need is likely to take the form of the need for one or more of the following:
>
> i) the provision of special means of access to the curriculum through special equipment, facilities or resources, modification of the physical environment or specialist teaching techniques;
> ii) the provision of a special or modified curriculum;
> iii) particular attention to the social structure and emotional climate in which education takes place. (p. 41)

These are in fact forms of provision, and beg the question 'Why do children need them?'. And it is the answer to this question that identifies educational need. Educational needs are the skills, attitudes, knowledge and personal qualities that we wish children to learn. The above items from *A Curriculum for All* and the Warnock Report are all suitable forms of provision to facilitate learning in desired areas.

Educational research has also drawn attention to this problem. One study reviewed submissions made by LEAs. The researchers highlighted a number of documents where this distinction between need and provision had not been appreciated. Being able to distinguish between needs and provision has implications for assessing and reporting on children's progress, under the assessment procedure introduced under the 1981 Education Act (see Chapter 4).

What is required is a move towards greater clarity in defining the educational needs of all children and the appropriate provision to meet them, and less time spent on the largely administrative issue of whether those needs are 'special' educational needs. Part of the problem is that while it is not difficult to find definitions of what 'special' educational needs are, there are few unambiguous definitions of what 'educational' needs are. That assistance is required in this task was illustrated by Neville Bennett and his colleagues (1984) through their research, reported in *The Quality of Pupil Learning Experiences*.

In any mainstream class of 25–30 children, pupils will have a wide range of attainments. Meeting a diverse range of needs is inevitably problematic and it has been well documented that teachers face difficulties in individualizing instruction to meet the needs of all children. This is highlighted by what happens to those children who cannot engage in the same learning experiences as other children in the class. In particular, concern is expressed over whether the low or high attainers are having their needs met. Bennett and his colleagues worked with sixteen teachers, all of whom were defined as 'good' by advisers. They found that:

- in top infants only 40 per cent of children were on appropriate tasks;
- this figure dropped to 30 per cent in first year juniors;
- tasks were never judged to be too easy;
- high achievers spent more time on practice tasks than learning to apply or generalize their knowledge;
- low achievers, who invariably require extensive practice, spent very little time on such activities. Instead they spent most of their time being introduced to new material.

There are many children whose needs are not being met. By focusing our attention on those seen to have difficulties, we are inadvertently concealing the much larger problems of finding ways to meet the needs of all children, not only those perceived to be experiencing difficulties. Appropriate provision is lacking across the board for many children, not just those for whom a statement is deemed appropriate. How we look at a classroom, whether we see some children as experiencing a learning difficulty or not, whether we focus on the needs of all the children or not, are perceptions which are underpinned by our personal theories of teaching and learning. These in turn reflect our values and beliefs, an area which will now be considered.

Values

Our educational philosophies are underpinned by our values, our beliefs, our understanding of the world. The myths we promulgate and our choice of language imply values. We see it in language that is sexist or racist, and I have argued in this chapter that we have to become more sensitive to discriminatory practices and language with respect to children's achievements.

Our values and beliefs provide us with a template for our perceptions of the world; they inform our choice of language usage and inspire the educational philosophies we attempt to implement in the classroom. Seeing the concept of special educational needs as a problem in managing children's learning has inevitable consequences for the nature of educational practice, whether it be related to future research, to selecting suitable teaching approaches, to assessing children's learning or to the training of teachers.

While there may be a general willingness to acknowledge that values underpin practice, often they are not discussed or their significance is not fully appreciated. Educational debate frequently revolves around the nature of evidence, rather than the values on which that evidence is founded. This has been clearly illustrated in debates about falling standards and teaching methods. Discussion has tended to focus on the available evidence, with one side asserting the validity of their data in response to heavy criticism from opponents. However, it seems unlikely that evidence can ever satisfactorily resolve the dispute. Evidence merely serves to camouflage the values underpinning the discussion, which rarely get aired but which may in reality lie at the heart of educational differences.

Through focusing on evidence, opportunities to explore shared values between apparent protagonists are rare. Yet it may be that seemingly opposing stances are underpinned by shared values. Debates about different approaches to curriculum development, pedagogical styles and systems of evaluation cannot be resolved without recognizing the values that influence the discussion.

A commitment to promoting equal opportunities in all aspects of school life will determine the nature of children's learning experiences. Similarly, a belief that the concept of special needs is both discriminatory and anachronistic will lead to educational practice which is qualitatively different to that where this is not held to be the case. It is our values and beliefs that create our expectations for what children might achieve and subsequently influence our understanding of the teaching, learning and assessment processes.

The arguments presented in this chapter can be summarized by suggesting that we should:

- challenge the assumptions underpinning special education, particularly the 'one in five';
- highlight the ways in which our everyday language may be discriminatory;
- focus on what children have achieved;
- become more effective in identifying the educational needs of all children.

The way these issues are faced has major implications for how children learn, how their progress is assessed on a continuous basis by teachers and how their behaviour is managed. These implications are addressed in the following chapters.

Chapter 3

UNDERSTANDING AND MANAGING CHILDREN'S LEARNING

Introduction

This chapter explores the basis of the myth (introduced in Chapter 2) that children with special educational needs have a difficulty in learning. It examines the nature of children's difficulties, the aims of teaching and the means by which educational goals can be achieved. It is argued that all children require similar educational experiences and opportunities, although those who cause concern may require additional planning and preparation time. Furthermore, it is suggested that the principles of 'good teaching' and 'good special needs teaching' are the same. Teachers who are able to meet the demand of a diverse range of needs will be effective in meeting the needs of children seen to have difficulties. This principle was illustrated in a recent HMI survey (DES, 1989b) of pupils with special needs in ordinary schools. HMI noted that features of good practice were common to primary and secondary school and that these features 'applied to the teaching of all pupils, and not just those with SEN' (para. 26).

This chapter starts by considering the characteristics of children seen to have a difficulty in learning.

Characteristics of children with learning difficulties

Research suggests that children are more likely to be seen to have special needs if they experience problems in learning to read than if they have difficulties in other curriculum areas. If diagnosis of special needs were based on competence at playing the piano, cooking or sporting prowess, a very different population might be identified as requiring help with their learning. In some senses, everyone might be seen as having a learning difficulty at some time or another: we may regard ourselves as competent readers but might be inclined to revise our claims when required to make sense of tax forms, legal documents or a DIY manual.

Given that we tend to focus on certain areas of the curriculum, what draws children to our attention as having a difficulty in learning? Our perception may be that they:

- learn at a slower rate than their peers;
- have a difficulty in concentrating;
- seem to have difficulty in retaining new information;
- rarely complete set tasks;
- require more one-to-one attention;
- appear unable to follow instructions;
- attain in one or more subjects at a lower level than their peers.

Such behaviour is certainly consistent with having a difficulty in learning, but can it be attributed to other factors? This question can be examined through considering some implications for teachers of children having difficulties in learning.

When children experience problems, a teacher's ability to teach is openly challenged. On a day-to-day basis, it is usually assumed that children's educational experiences contribute to their successful learning. However, the evidence is rarely available to show that it was these experiences, and these experiences alone, that resulted in learning. In most instances, it cannot be demonstrated that children's daily classroom activities result in positive outcomes. When children fail to learn, however, we know that the school and home environments are not successfully facilitating learning. Teachers face the uncomfortable fact that, although we cannot state with complete confidence which experiences lead to successful learning, we know the ones which do not.

The starting point for many teachers when children are seen to fail is that 'these children have not made progress despite our most determined efforts'. There is a tendency to believe that, as all the other children have learned as intended, the teaching approaches adopted in the classroom have generally been successful. Thus, children fail to learn because they have a learning difficulty. A number of assumptions lie behind this belief.

It is assumed that all the children's opportunities for learning have been the same. Equally, it is felt that the same teaching environment automatically ensures the same learning experiences. Finally, and perhaps most importantly, it implies that everything possible has been done at a local authority, school and classroom level to ensure resources have been optimally organized to meet the children's educational needs. However, various studies provide grounds for challenging these assumptions.

Research by Neville Bennett and his colleagues (1984) found that on some occasions children were only on appropriate tasks approximately 40 per cent of the time. They also found that, while teachers were often able to judge when tasks were too difficult, they never judged tasks to be too easy. Also, tasks were often seen by the research team to be promoting different areas of learning to those intended by the teachers. Another study showed that a high level of class teaching is still taking place, implying that individual children are not having the curriculum geared to their particular needs. While whole-class teaching is a necessary means of organizing learning, there are also a number of occasions when it is inappropriate for meeting children's educational needs. There is sufficient evidence from this and other research to conclude that exposing children to the same curricular experiences as peers does not guarantee that their needs are being met.

Children with learning difficulties or teachers with teaching difficulties?

So if it is not children that have learning difficulties, are we talking about teachers with teaching difficulties? In Chapter 1, when we looked at developments in special education, we saw how the impact of psychology on education has concentrated attention on the individual differences between children and on the explanations for their occurrence. As a result, a failure to learn has invariably been attributed to the characteristics of the child.

Perhaps this is inevitable, given the way most teachers are introduced to psychology on their teacher education courses. Much of the psychology studied is exclusively concerned with children and their development. This emphasis helps to create notions of what is 'normal development'. Consequently, when children experience either learning or behavioural difficulties, something is seen to be 'wrong' with their development rather than with any aspect of their learning environment.

More recently, however, educational psychology has focused on the nature of classroom interactions. This perspective advocates that teachers should begin to examine their own behaviour in the classroom as a starting point for positive classroom interactions. We know from our own experiences as pupils how important the learning environment is in facilitating progress. We probably tended to be interested in subjects taught by teachers we preferred and to be less positive about lessons when we disliked the teacher. We can therefore speculate that key factors in determining whether or not children are going to experience difficulties are subject content and the quality of pupil–teacher relationships.

This new approach encourages teachers to become more reflective in examining relationships in the classroom and the nature of children's successful and unsuccessful learning experiences. Teachers have to acknowledge their responsibility to facilitate children's successful classroom learning. Asserting this position does not ignore the significance of children's personal development or the skills, attributes and qualities they bring to school. However, it is important to recognize that these provide a starting point for planning classroom activities, rather than either a barrier to future learning or a potential explanation for failure.

A consequence of teachers' being reflective is that statements about children have to be considered in the light of what they also imply about teachers. Postman and Weingartner, in their widely read educational polemic of the late 1960s, *Teaching as a Subversive Activity*, addressed this issue. They believe that comments about children are initially and indirectly revealing something about the teacher:

> For example, we say 'John is stupid' or 'Helen is smart' as if 'stupidity' and 'smartness' were characteristics of John and Helen. A literal translation of 'John is stupid' (that is its most scientific meaning) might go something like this: 'When I perceive John's behaviour, I am disappointed or distressed or frustrated or disgusted. The sentence I use to express my perceptions and evaluations of these events is John is stupid'. (Postman and Weingartner, 1969, pp. 101–2)

Our statements reflect our attitudes, beliefs and perceptions of children. To attribute a failure to learn to the personal characteristics of children means that, to some extent, we can avoid accepting responsibility for that failure. Perhaps one reason why psychology has rarely been presented to student teachers as a platform for self-appraisal and self-reflection is that it might thus be found too threatening.

Some children may fail to learn because of the way they have been taught. This view was reflected in two recent publications from the National Curriculum Council:

> Special educational needs are not just a reflection of pupils' inherent difficulties; they are often related to factors within schools which can prevent or exacerbate some problems. (NCC, 1989a, para. 5, p. 1)

> The interaction between the pupil and the school, including its curriculum, can also lead to learning difficulties. We need, therefore, to define the conditions in which children and young people can learn successfully and to ensure that the school curriculum enables these to be met. (NCC, 1989b, p. 1)

What are the implications for teachers who:

- accept that the learning environment may contribute in some way to a child's failure to learn;

- are willing to accept responsibility for that failure;
- take steps to ensure that the child experiences success in the future?

Maybe these teachers would acknowledge to the children whose progress causes concern that they are not sure where the difficulties lie. They might ask the children for their observations and opinions about how they are being taught and reassure them that it is not their problem. It is a difficulty for the teachers to resolve.

Although this scenario may seem improbable, it represents the alternative end of the continuum to the one which suggests that there is something 'wrong' with the child. Perhaps a more fruitful starting point, with fewer recriminations for teachers and children, sees both parties as needing to collaborate and negotiate in order to try to establish patterns of classroom organization and learning experiences that facilitate optimal progress.

The purpose of the discussion so far is to illustrate that our understanding about whether children experience learning difficulties is influenced by a range of perceptions. Typically, the reason cited has been the individual characteristics of the child, whereas the alternative interpretation suggests that it is teachers who are presented with a teaching difficulty. Three key points arise from this polarized stance about the nature of learning difficulties.

In one sense, it is questionable whether any useful purpose is served by debating the issues at length. What is of primary importance is the steps taken to overcome difficulties. The scope of teaching should not be limited by perceptions of what it is thought children are capable of achieving. This topic was addressed in Chapter 2, but it is worth repeating that the DES report *Curriculum Organisation and Classroom Practice in Primary Schools: a discussion paper* (DES 1992) identified having higher expectations as one of the key issues to be addressed by teachers.

Equally, whatever the source of the difficulties, *a problem exists when a teacher is concerned about a child's learning*

45

and progress in school. The task confronting teachers is how best to meet the child's needs and promote successful learning experiences in the future. Meeting a range of educational needs within a single classroom is a complex and highly skilled process. It challenges the professional competence of teachers and those within the education system to find a set of satisfactory outcomes from a range of differing perspectives.

Finally, what is required is teachers who approach the task of overcoming a child's lack of progress with an open mind, with a willingness to experiment and to explore all potential routes to success. It is probably not the internalized models of children's learning that matter so much as the beliefs, attitudes and values of the teachers working with those pupils. Perhaps the essence of good 'special education' is the willingness to accept uncertainties, take responsibility for children's learning and gather evidence on progress in response to a variety of teaching approaches.

The next section looks at the ways children's learning can be promoted. It starts by discussing issues seen to have arisen from past practice and concludes by introducing strategies by which difficulties may be overcome.

Promoting children's learning: learning from the past

It has been said that there are only two things wrong in 'special education': one is that it is not special, and the other that it is not education. Some of the factors that gave rise to such a cynical view of special education were reflected in the HMI survey (DES, 1989b) of pupils with special educational needs in ordinary schools. While HMI felt that the quality of work in 55 per cent of the teaching sessions seen for primary pupils was satisfactory or better, this obviously implied that the quality of work was less than satisfactory in 45 per cent of the sessions. In secondary schools, the quality of work was considered to be satisfactory in only half the observed lessons.

Work provided for children did not meet their specific needs. Activities were either too easy or too difficult and engaged them in mechanical copying exercises. Many schools in the sample provided children with activities which were narrow in their focus and gave them neither a broad curriculum nor a variety of different types of learning experiences, so children tended to get a regular diet of 'basic skills'. In mathematics, there were large numbers of computation exercises, which some children were completing incorrectly without appropriate materials to help them to understand the number relationships involved. Finally, some schools did not have a clearly articulated policy on teaching special needs which had been developed by specialist staff through consultation and negotiation with senior management and other colleagues.

Many of these criticisms have been noted in different contexts. They address the following concerns:

- the nature of the curriculum;
- the development of 'packages'.

The nature of the curriculum

The majority of children with special educational needs are taught in mainstream schools. In the past they have invariably received a different curriculum and different range of learning experiences to those of their peers, particularly when they have been taught on a withdrawal basis. Children have learned in a fairly formal manner, with very little direct involvement in negotiating and managing aspects of their own learning. Skills have been taught in isolation without appropriate references to the contexts in which they were to be used. Finally, children with difficulties have often been given individualized work which demands considerable teacher supervision time. Teachers often report that there is not enough time to give children with difficulties the individual time they require.

Children need to engage in a variety of activities to indicate that they have learned successfully. It is not sufficient for young children to demonstrate that tasks can be performed accurately, or are remembered over time. They need to learn to generalize their knowledge and apply it to real-life problems and situations. They also require opportunities to work independently and co-operatively with peers. When given a balanced range of learning experiences, children who have difficulties neither require nor will benefit from high levels of direct pupil–teacher contact time.

The development of 'packages'

Many of the problems just described were associated with the use of training 'packages'. These materials promoted forms of continuous, curriculum-based teacher assessment. They typically contained basic skills curricula, checklists of pupil attainments, guidance on teaching methods and advice on recording pupil progress. They were invariably grafted on to existing practice. They donated curricula, or implied them through basic skills checklists, unrelated to the mainstream curricula. Teachers were, therefore, often asked to do something different for the small number of children experiencing difficulties.

A research project which examined provision for children with special needs in six LEAs drew attention to these issues. The researchers identified one authority which provided detailed materials for training teachers in mainstream schools in various teaching approaches, developed extensively in special education contexts. Teachers saw them as something different to everyday practice and felt they were only for those children with difficulties.

Undoubtedly meeting the needs of all the children in a class is demanding. It requires flexibility, knowledge of the curriculum, being skilled in a variety of teaching methods and a commitment to achieving success with all children. Previous experience suggests that there are no ready-made solutions or materials that easily overcome children's difficulties. Success is most likely to be achieved through applying the principles of good practice to meeting the needs of all children, irrespective of their initial attainments.

Effective teaching and learning

This section addresses the following topics:

- aims;
- developing the curriculum;
- identifying educational needs;
- objectives for children's intended learning outcomes;
- teaching and learning;
- feedback;
- evaluation.

Aims

The aims of education for children seen to experience difficulties are the same as for other children. The Warnock Committee suggested that one aim is to enable each child to 'enter the world after formal education is over as an active participant of society and a responsible contributor to it capable of achieving as much independence as possible' (DES, 1978, p. 5). The purpose and goals of education are the same for all children.

Earlier discussion has indicated that the learning environment could be a source of children's difficulties. If this is so, it is only reasonable to conclude that a child has a difficulty after demonstrating that nothing more could be done to improve the quality of teaching offered. Thus, given existing knowledge about how to teach, every attempt should be made to ensure that the most effective curricula, patterns of classroom organization and teaching approaches are adopted to teach children who present problems. The only way of knowing whether children have a difficulty in learning is through teaching them.

It is assumed that differences in attainments can be overcome, but that less time is available to teach children all they need to learn. Children of 7 who have not yet started to read have to catch up with their peers. Those who are noticeably behind, therefore, need to be taught 'more in less time' if their standard of reading is to be the same as that of other children by the time they are 11 and ready to transfer to a secondary school. The aim of teaching is to '*bridge the gap*' in attainments as far as is possible in the time available.

When the learning environment, rather than the child, becomes the focus of attention, the key question changes from 'How do children learn?' to 'What are the most effective ways of teaching?'. The former question is derived from views on child-centred education (introduced in Chapter 1), and rarely takes account of the teaching arrangements that contribute to children's learning. These are acknowledged by asking how we can teach more effectively.

So how might teachers promote positive, successful and rewarding experiences for children seen to be experiencing difficulties and enable them to bridge the curriculum gap?

Developing the curriculum

The curriculum has to fulfil two functions in relation to the children we are concerned about. It must help teachers to accelerate children's progress so that the curriculum gap can be bridged. It must also enable teachers to assess children's educational needs.

Bridging the curriculum gap. In special education two complementary curriculum approaches have been developed which fulfil the above aims: task analysis and direct instruction. Task analysis typically incorporates a three-step procedure which involves clarifying what is to be taught and ensuring appropriate curriculum progression. Children's learning experiences are arranged so that areas of the curriculum that might be easier to learn are presented before more demanding ones. Furthermore, it is anticipated that, in some instances, learning earlier skills and concepts will facilitate children's learning of later and potentially more complex areas of the curriculum.

Task analysis also makes provision for differentiating the curriculum so that learning experiences are geared to meet children's individual needs. This is achieved in one of two ways. Tasks and activities which are too difficult are changed so that they become accessible to the children seen to have difficulties. Alternatively, children with problems are given the same activity as peers, but are expected to complete work in a different way. So, for example, where they are asked to provide a written account of some work they have undertaken, those with difficulties might be expected to write less or present some of their responses in a pictorial format.

Direct instruction has made a significant contribution in enabling children to bridge the curriculum gap. When learning literacy and numeracy skills, there is a vast amount of information to be acquired. If each area of the curriculum were taught separately, there would be insufficient time to teach everything that needs to be learned. Children can bridge the curriculum gap through learning to generalize and apply their skills and knowledge to new areas of the curriculum. Many children who succeed at school learn how to generalize and apply newly acquired areas of learning on their own. However, others do not, for a variety of reasons, and these are often the children who experience difficulties. The task for the teacher, therefore, is to demonstrate to children how they can generalize and apply previous learning.

The premise of much educational theory has often been that children will learn to generalize and apply their knowledge at a developmentally appropriate time and should preferably learn to make the necessary connections for themselves. While many children achieve this, some need their teacher to intervene directly to help them to generalize and apply their knowledge, so they may catch up with their peers. Every avenue must be explored to facilitate learning, even when this means re-evaluating cherished views of teaching and learning.

The National Curriculum. The National Curriculum forms the basis of what all children are to be taught and is seen as an 'entitlement curriculum'. The 1988 Education Act requires all maintained schools, including special schools (but not hospital schools), to follow it. However, the Secretary of State for Education and Science may modify or withdraw parts of the National Curriculum and related assessment arrangements under certain circumstances.

At best, the National Curriculum provides a general framework in which teachers have to work. The principles of task analysis and direct instruction can readily be applied to the ways individual schools interpret and develop it to meet the educational needs of children with a diverse range of attainments. This is particularly so since the statements of attainment are frequently ambiguous, and no clear rationale has ever been offered for the curricular sequences offered. Further discussion on the National Curriculum and an example of how it can be developed for children experiencing difficulties are presented in Chapter 4 (pp. 65–70).

Assessment. Facilitating the process of continuous assessment and enabling teachers to accelerate children's learning are highly compatible aims in developing the curriculum. The purpose of the assessment process is to find out what children can learn *with existing resources and provision.* Teaching children to generalize and apply their learning should not require any more time than teachers feel is reasonable, given the other demands on their daily schedules. Details of the provision made to teach children felt to have difficulties are recorded, and contribute to the assessment of the child's educational needs, through indicating what children learn with current resources. Chapter 4 discusses in detail how children's learning is assessed and highlights the relationship between teaching, learning and assessment.

Identifying educational needs

Educational needs embrace the knowledge, skills and concepts which are necessary for the development of children's learning, and refer to what needs to be learned next. This decision is based on establishing what children already know and can already do. Needs are identified through systematic observation and assessment within the children's everyday learning environment, and within a clearly defined framework over a period of time. Once existing attainments have been determined, decisions can be taken about what to teach in the future and the most appropriate forms of provision to meet educational needs.

Objectives for children's intended learning outcomes

Objectives clarify what the learner must do to demonstrate that learning has occurred, and are usually identified before any teaching takes place. Recent research suggests that clarifying activities and intended outcomes to pupils significantly improves their learning. Children understand what is expected and teachers can assess progress.

However, concerns have been expressed about articulating learning outcomes before any teaching occurs. The influence of child-centred education led many teachers to argue that objectives cannot be prescribed with certainty, since what children learn depends on their previous knowledge and understanding of the world. It is argued that, while we may set up learning opportunities for children, we cannot be certain what they subsequently learn.

Even where teachers are committed to, and thus formulate, learning objectives in advance, children inevitably learn many things incidentally. Teachers should accept that learning can, and will, take place in ways that had not been anticipated, and should be sufficiently flexible to recognize that on some occasions prespecifying objectives is neither desirable nor possible. It should also be emphasized that stating objectives in a clear and precise way does not predetermine choice of teaching methods, which can be and frequently are related to a range of approaches.

What is less open to dispute is that learning outcomes are determined through observing behaviour. The dilemma to be confronted, irrespective of whether objectives are prespecified, is which behaviour is consistent with a child having 'learned' a particular concept. This is not a difficulty *created* by either systematic observation of behaviour or clarifying learning outcomes, but one *illustrated* by such an approach. How do we know whether children have acquired important language, mathematical or scientific concepts, except by seeing whether their knowledge and understanding can be applied in different contexts and are manifest in a number of different ways?

Teaching and learning

The aim of teaching is to enable children to generalize and apply the concepts, knowledge and skills they learn to real-life situations, both inside and outside the classroom. Too often in the past, as has often been noted by HMI, special education for children with learning difficulties has focused narrowly on isolated skill development outside the broader context of skill application. Within special education, the instructional hierarchy of Haring and Eaton (1978; described in Solity and Bull, 1987, and Solity and Raybould, 1988) emphasizes a range of learning opportunities that children should experience. It stresses that children who have become accurate and fluent in the use of skills must be encouraged to generalize and apply their knowledge. Furthermore, research into the hierarchy indicates that teaching methods need to vary for each stage of learning. The methods that are effective when introducing new skills and knowledge will not necessarily be the most effective in enabling children to apply what they have learned.

Attention therefore needs to be drawn to two different aspects of the teaching and learning processes. Learning can occur through a child's engagement in a range of complementary activities designed to promote the development of a particular concept or skill. These activities emphasize the importance of children learning through first-hand experience. Typically, this process requires children to work out for themselves the rules for generalizing skills and concepts they have learned. Such approaches can be retained and encouraged when children make acceptable progress which enables them to 'bridge the curriculum gap'.

However, should this level of success not be achieved, teachers need to adopt a different role in the learning process. Here teachers attempt to convey skills and knowledge through more formal teaching methods, with fewer opportunities for children to initiate their own learning experiences. Under these circumstances, the aim is to ensure that the principles for generalizing concepts or skills are identified overtly, and their intrinsic rules demonstrated and taught directly to children.

Specific teaching methods have been adopted which maximize the impact of pupil–teacher contact time. They have a number of features which aim to accelerate children's progress. Strategies are adopted to ensure that:

- activities are always at an appropriate level of difficulty for the children;
- children are taught for brief periods daily;
- children are totally involved in the learning experience;
- children quickly experience considerable success in areas that in the past had proved difficult.

Specific techniques may involve:

- showing children how to perform activities before they undertake them on their own (known as *modelling*);
- doing activities at the same time as the child (known as *leading*);
- giving children various kinds of help (in a systematic manner, so that their impact on learning is noted) to enable them to perform activities on their own (known as *prompting*);
- giving children opportunities to *practise*;
- giving children opportunities to '*test*' themselves to see that tasks and activities can be performed without any help from the teacher;
- using errors as an important source of *feedback*, which enables difficulties to be identified and overcome.

Where possible, children with difficulties should:

- understand the purpose of teaching and the nature of their activities;
- be given similar learning experiences to those of their peers;
- be encouraged to work co-operatively;

- negotiate aspects of their own learning;
- be involved in assessing and evaluating their progress.

In reality, when the stages of the hierarchy form the basis of learning, children are taught by approaches typically associated with both child-centred and teacher-directed education. The latter are most appropriate in the early stages of acquiring new skills, knowledge and concepts, with child-centred approaches being adopted to facilitate children's application of previous learning.

Feedback

Giving children feedback on their learning and reviewing progress are essential features of effective teaching. Within child-centred learning contexts, teachers help children to interpret and structure their experiences. This is an essential corollary of task setting, where a range of opportunities and learning outcomes is made available. The reviewing procedure helps children to assimilate aspects of learning and to extend the application of concepts to new areas.

Feedback fulfils a very similar role within the more teacher-directed approaches described above. When appropriate, children are given details about their progress so that they can begin to appreciate that they are learning. Feedback takes several forms, but usually occurs through discussion with the teacher and, where appropriate, is emphasized and made 'tangible' by being presented visually (for example, in graphs and charts). Feedback aims to show children that they are learning by comparing current achievements with past levels of attainment.

Evaluation

Evaluation identifies those teaching strategies which promote successful learning for individual children and those which do not. Implicit in this process is an approach to evaluation based on teachers' objectives. The nature of evaluation is curriculum-based, continuous in character, and rests on assessing children's responses to teaching procedures over a period of time. This is discussed in more detail in Chapter 4.

This chapter has discussed the challenges posed to teachers when faced with children who are seen to experience a difficulty in learning. It has argued that the aim of teaching is to enable children who are behind in their learning to bridge the curriculum gap that exists between them and their peers. This can only be realized when children are given opportunities to generalize and apply their skills, knowledge and concepts.

Effective teaching has a number of features, including an assumption that it is the teacher's responsibility to ensure that learning takes place. When progress does not meet expectations, the learning environment is examined rather than the child. Pupils' involvement is seen as essential in negotiating, initiating and understanding the nature of their learning experiences. Teachers as professionals need to keep the teaching and learning processes under review, through systematically observing, monitoring and evaluating the balance and range of provision.

Children respond differently to the ways they are taught. What works for one child may not work for another. Equally, an individual child needs a variety of approaches. The effective teacher should therefore be conversant with a range of approaches which can facilitate children's learning, a point emphasized in the report by Alexander, Rose and Woodhead (DES, 1992). While some patterns of classroom organization and methods of promoting learning may well predominate, this should not be to the exclusion of alternatives. The instructional hierarchy also emphasizes that different methods are necessary for each stage of learning.

The chapter has concentrated on facilitating learning in areas where children are seen to be failing. Effective teaching recognizes achievements in all areas of the curriculum, including those where difficulties are being experienced. It also extends beyond the parameters of the National Curriculum and encompasses the personal qualities what we wish children to learn, which are the subject of Chapter 5.

The introduction of the National Curriculum presents teachers with a new scenario in which to consider their effectiveness. There is increased pressure on teachers to ensure that children reach specific levels of attainment, and for their progress to be systematically assessed through both continuous teacher assessments and, more formally, national standard assessment tasks. Teachers are concerned as to how they will meet the demands being made while at the same time providing children with a stimulating curriculum. If children fail to make satisfactory progress it will be tempting to argue that they do so through having learning difficulties. It will be at these times that teachers' beliefs and values will be of greater importance than educational rhetoric in determining the educational opportunities which children are offered.

Chapter 4

ASSESSING CHILDREN'S LEARNING

Introduction

This chapter examines various concepts of assessment in relation to children with special educational needs. It starts by exploring the aims of the assessment process, introduces three different methods of assessment and relates these to both teacher and Key Stage assessments. The chapter concludes by discussing the statutory assessment procedure which was introduced under the 1981 Education Act. This is initiated when children are felt to have needs which cannot be met through existing school resources – that is, when they are perceived to have special educational needs.

When children attend school we naturally want to know what they have learned. The means by which we find this out is referred to as the process of assessment. Assessment is sometimes seen as unrelated to teaching and learning, but in reality they are inextricably linked. It is difficult to assess learning without also considering what children were intended to learn and how they were taught. Assessment plays a central role in the classroom, enabling teachers to plan appropriate learning experiences for children.

Earlier chapters have indicated that in the past there have been differences in the ways that children have had their needs assessed. Certainly the IQ test was still being widely used to assess children's suitability for special education when its limitations in relation to the 11-plus were recognized. The implementation of the 1988 Education Act has focused attention on the most appropriate ways of assessing learning to facilitate children's progress in school. The new legislation and the assessment procedures it encourages emphasize the need to have a common approach to assessing the needs of all children. However, the way we assess depends on the questions to be answered and our aims in assessing children's learning.

The aims of assessment

The principle aim of assessment is to find out whether children are learning. The answer to the question 'Are children learning?' is influenced by the frequency of assessment, how information is collected, how it is to be interpreted and whom the information is for. The way these issues are addressed has both methodological and moral implications. It is helpful to start by examining the aims of assessment for the class teacher.

Class teachers need regular information on how children are progressing, in order to plan future lessons and activities. Without feedback, it is difficult to provide appropriate learning experiences, where new activities are built on existing knowledge. The more frequent the assessment, the greater the likelihood that teaching is geared to meeting children's needs. Regular assessment can also inform children of their progress: feedback helps them to appreciate the extent of this through examining errors and providing constructive guidance on how learning can be improved. This has increasingly been shown to be an effective way of sustaining interest and motivation.

Assessment of this kind also has other equally valuable dimensions for the class teacher. Frequent monitoring of children's progress builds up a picture of how individual children learn and highlights the most successful teaching approaches. It is through the process of assessment that teachers develop their own expertise and understanding of how children learn best. So in a sense, assessment of children's learning is also an assessment of the effectiveness of teaching.

Assessment functions at an informal and a formal level. It is informal when there is no documented evidence to support teacher decisions, perhaps because there is too much information to record. Assessment becomes more formal when records are kept which detail the salient aspects of children's learning. These are necessary to provide a documented profile of children's academic achievements. At different stages during the learning process it is necessary to establish and to record just what individual children have learned at any given moment in time. This provides teachers with evidence on both children's learning and the effectiveness of their teaching. These assessments are particularly important for children seen to have difficulties and provide invaluable records for colleagues, parents, governors and members of the LEA.

Methods of assessment

There are two recognized forms of assessment used by teachers in their more formal role as assessors of children's learning. These are known as norm- and criterion-referenced assessment. A third, but less well-established, approach is ipsative assessment. This is probably the most useful when it comes to informing teachers about the effectiveness of their teaching and providing a basis for assessing children's learning. It is most valuable when attempting to ascertain the nature of children's difficulties and compiling reports for LEAs. Such reports offer teacher opinion and advice, which form part of the statutory assessment of children's special educational needs. This section on methods of assessment starts by examining norm- and criterion-referenced assessment before considering ipsative assessment.

Norm-referenced assessment

Norm-referenced assessment is designed to compare one child's performance with those of other children. It is probably the most familiar form of assessment to many. Children's development from birth is compared to established developmental norms. Within minutes of being born, children undergo their first normative assessment (the AGPAR test) as they are checked by midwives and rated on a ten-point

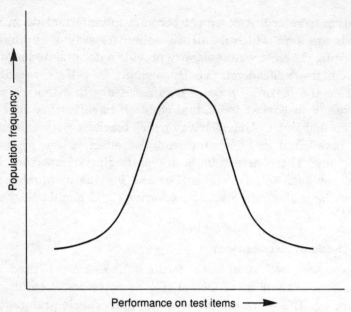

Figure 4.1 The normal distribution

scale. The rates at which children grow, talk, walk, etc. are all assessed on scales of normative development. There is cause for concern when development in any area does not conform to the predicted patterns. By the time children start school, parents are aware of the process of normative assessment and possibly expect to receive normative information about their child's progress.

Norm-referenced assessment in schools uses commercially prepared normative tests. These are specially designed to yield results which follow the normal distribution (see Figure 4.1). Normative tests are used because they discriminate between children and enable teachers to compare the performance of children in their class with each other and against expected standards. So they tell teachers whether children are doing as well as other children, but they have a number of limitations.

Norm-referenced tests are not curriculum related and so do not inform teachers about what children have learned or what they need to learn next. They can usually only be given once every six months, which means that they are often only given once each academic year. They do not help teachers highlight areas of strength or weakness and so are probably of limited use when it comes to regular teacher assessments. Thus, although norm-referenced assessment can provide data on comparable groups of children in different parts of the country, it is of limited use in relation to determining the educational needs of individual children.

Criterion-referenced assessment

Criterion-referenced assessment, on the other hand, aims to find out what children have and have not learned in specific areas of the curriculum. It does not produce scores which enable comparisons to be made between pupils. Used positively, it concentrates on children's achievements and identifies what they have learned. However, it does not provide details on children's progress over time, or on how pupils learn best or on how to teach most effectively. Neither does it relate curriculum content and choice of teaching methods to pupils' learning. Criterion-referenced assessment can, therefore, be useful in telling you what children have achieved, but not the conditions or circumstances that most successfully facilitate learning.

Ipsative assessment

Ipsative assessment focuses on what children have or have not learned and then enables comparisons to be made between current and previous performance levels. It aims to provide information on children's rate of progress and the circumstances under which they learn best, and guidance to teachers on the effectiveness of their own teaching. It is particularly helpful in relation to children seen to be experiencing difficulties, since it fulfils the aims of assessment outlined earlier, as well as addressing teachers' concerns about children's difficulties.

Teachers are concerned about children who are behind in their learning and generally want to know how far behind their peers children are, and the reasons for this. Is poor progress due to learning difficulties or other factors? Under these circumstance, ipsative assessment aims to establish what children can learn with the available, existing provision and whether they will be able to bridge the gap between their attainments and those of peers. Within teacher assessment, the central issue is not so much 'Does this child have a learning difficulty?' as 'What can this child learn when offered systematic teaching? Which approaches promote learning? Can the child's educational needs be met satisfactorily with existing resources and provision?'. As discussed in Chapter 3, these questions need to be addressed before considering whether poor progress can be attributed to a difficulty in learning.

The three methods of assessment have different roles within the teacher and Key Stage assessments. Teachers' preferred choices of assessment method depend to some extent on their own attitudes and values and what they feel they can achieve in their own classrooms. Both teacher and Key Stage assessments for children with special needs have to be considered within the context of current thinking about special education. As was suggested in Chapter 2, this is heavily influenced by educational myths and the language through which they are promulgated.

The emphasis in special education is to examine the overall circumstances under which children experience difficulties. This incorporates an assessment of the learning environment, the teaching styles and the curriculum, as well as the attributes of the child. Teacher assessment is the essential component in gaining a full understanding and appreciation of children's educational needs. The next section raises some key issues concerning teacher assessment, considers the assessment of children with difficulties and relates this to the principles and procedures for assessing the educational needs of all the children in a class, not only those seen to experience problems.

Teacher assessment

Teachers make hundreds of daily assessments about children's learning. They assess the level of progress being achieved and the suitability of teaching approaches, together with making a range of decisions about children's social interactions. Much of the forthcoming information remains in teachers' heads and thus represents what was referred to earlier as the informal assessment process. Teachers need to make the information from these assessments more open and accessible. How can assessments be undertaken which yield information that both informs future teaching and provides a systematic record of children's learning?

The focus in teacher assessment should be that it:

- is derived from everyday practice;
- is curriculum-based;
- involves children;
- concentrates on children's achievements rather than their ability;
- is concerned with gathering evidence in the classroom about the nature of children's learning and their responses to different teaching approaches.

Teacher assessment can thus be seen to draw on the principles of ipsative and criterion-referenced assessment rather than normative assessment.

How, then, might teachers begin to collect reliable and valid evidence on children's learning which is curriculum based, carried out regularly and involves children? The starting point in this process depends on how tasks are set.

Setting tasks for children's learning

Advice has been forthcoming from a number of influential sources about setting tasks for children's learning. The process of task setting provides the basis for collecting evidence on progress and, to be effective, emphasizes the need to assess what can be observed directly. The way tasks are set may or may not facilitate this. It is suggested that the statements of attainment in the National Curriculum need to be translated into a range of tasks and activities to help ensure that intended learning outcomes are clarified and unambiguous.

While the National Curriculum has been seen by some to represent a detailed series of statements about what children should learn, this underestimates the different interpretations possible of learning outcomes. It is perhaps best viewed as a framework within which teachers have to work, but where they may still retain considerable autonomy over how they teach and even what they teach. The statements of attainment are in many instances vague and ambiguous, and need to be translated into realistic objectives for children's learning. Different teachers may well offer very different learning experiences because they have alternative interpretations of the statements of attainment.

For example, when teaching mathematics, level 1 of attainment target 2 states that children should be able to 'count, read, write and order numbers to at least 10; know that the size of a set is given by the last number in the count'. This statement could yield a variety of different tasks which could be offered to establish whether children had achieved this level of attainment. For example, children might have to:

- *count* by rote from 1 to 10;
- *count* the number of objects in a single set, such as

1	1	1	1	1	1

- *count* the number of objects in two sets individually and then count the number of objects in both sets in order to state how many objects there are *altogether* – for example,

Set 1

1	1	1	1

Set 2

1	1

This task demands that the child names the first object in the second set as 1 when *counting* the sets separately and as 5 when *counting* how many altogether. Furthermore, the child indicates on three separate occasions that the last number in the count indicates the number in a set;

- skip *count* – for example,
  2, 4, 6, 8, 10
- *count* on (and backwards) from a given number;

- *read* numbers when they appear in the following sequences:
  0, 1, 2, 3, 4, 5, 6, 7, 8, 9, 10
  8, 3, 1, 6, 7, 0, 5, 9, 2, 10, 4
- *write* numbers from dictation when they are read out in order and in a random sequence. In addition, children could *write* the numbers which are missing in the 1–10 sequence:
  4, –, 2, 9, –, –, 7, 6, –, 1, 8
- *order* numbers – for example,
  5, 9, 2, 10, 4, 7, 6, 1, 0, 3, 8

The above interpretation of the statement of attainment requires the child to complete over ten tasks.

This can be contrasted to the advice given to schools by the School Examinations and Assessment Council (SEAC) in their booklet to help teachers complete their teacher assessments (SEAC, 1992). The above statement of attainment is represented by only four different tasks, with each task possibly being less demanding than the ones just introduced. In the SEAC materials children are given five cards with a number written on and have to:

- set out the cards in *order*;
- *read* out the numbers;
- *write* down the numbers from 1 to 10;
- *count* the number of cards from a pile given by the teacher.

There are considerable differences between the two interpretations. Children may be able to complete the tasks suggested by SEAC and be said to have reached level 1, but still not be able to do the alternative series of tasks.

This example has been selected to illustrate the point that many statements of attainment can be open to different interpretations. The National Curriculum documents require a considerable amount of discussion and interpretation before they can be used effectively in schools.

Previous attempts to describe learning in more concrete terms than suggested by written statements of intent have involved the use of behavioural objectives. They tried to describe children's learning outcomes in terms of actions to be observed, the conditions under which activities were to be performed and criteria to indicate whether learning had taken place. A number of psychologists have advocated the use of behavioural objectives, particularly within special education, but they have been criticized. It is argued that they lead to a narrowing of the curriculum and fail to provide meaningful, purposeful and stimulating learning experiences.

Nevertheless, the School Examinations and Assessment Council (SEAC, 1989) and recent research in primary education have highlighted the importance of setting clear goals for assessing learning. Unless teachers know what they intend children to learn during the year, both individually and as a class, they cannot assess whether they themselves or their children have achieved these objectives.

Interestingly the SEAC advice on teacher assessment (SEAC, 1992) involves the use of behavioural objectives, although the term does not appear in the written literature sent to schools. It may well be that SEAC have decided to offer schools clearer and more structured guidance on assessment in response to past criticisms and evidence gathered when monitoring how teacher assessments were being conducted.

Much of what has been learned in the past when adopting an objectives approach to curriculum development can be helpful in guiding future practice to ensure that children are offered a broad and balanced curriculum. In general, the recent literature on specifying children's learning outcomes in clear, observable terms can be seen to have recognized some of the limitations of previous practice and drawn attention to the directions to be pursued in the future. The traditional dislike of behavioural objectives in mainstream education and the negative references made in many of the books currently available to student teachers are unfortunate, since effective curriculum-based assessment requires that tasks are defined in operational terms.

If it is recognized that a focus on observable behaviour enables teachers to ascertain that children are learning, it will be important that previous experience is acknowledged to ensure that the curriculum is neither trivialized nor undermined. The task to be faced now is to overcome the problems associated with earlier applications of an objectives approach so that children experience a broad and balanced curriculum, even though learning outcomes are specified in observable terms. To achieve this goal requires:

- having a framework for describing children's learning;
- identifying a process of assessment for all children, and not just those experiencing difficulties.

A framework for describing children's learning

A recent HMI (DES, 1990) report on the teaching and learning of language and literacy commented that a clear agreement about the criteria for progressing from one area of learning to another was an essential prerequisite of effective assessment and record-keeping. Researchers in the UK and USA have covered similar ground and offer similar guidance about the nature and range of children's learning experiences.

It is argued that tasks should be selected for children with respect to the learning they will help promote. Activities should be prepared which:

- *introduce* new ideas, skills, procedures and knowledge;
- require children to *invent* or *discover* an idea for themselves;
- enable children to develop their *accuracy* and *fluency* in learning new skills and knowledge;
- check that children *remember* newly acquired skills, concepts and knowledge over time, even though there has been no further teaching on these areas;
- help children to *discriminate* newly learned skills, concepts and knowledge from previously learned skills, concepts and knowledge;
- promote children's *application* of skills, concepts and knowledge to new problems.

Criteria for progressing from one task to another are implied by the different activities. Children are expected to become accurate, develop fluency and remember over time before learning how to apply their existing knowledge in different contexts and to real-life problems.

Learning experiences on these lines were recommended for all children in the Cockcroft Report (DES, 1982) on teaching mathematics. The report stated that 'all pupils need opportunities to practise skills and routines which have been acquired recently, and to consolidate those which they already possess, so that these may be available for use in problem solving and investigational work' (p. 73).

Recognizing the full range of learning experiences on which children should become engaged should prevent learning being trivialized, and should enable children to become successful in generalizing and applying their skills and knowledge to real-life problems. In addition, it is important that all children in a class, irrespective of their existing level of achievement, should have opportunities to generalize and apply their learning. In the past, children who have been seen to experience difficulties have tended to focus on the acquisition of early numeracy and literacy skills, without having opportunities to apply their skills and knowledge (Bennett *et al.*, 1984).

Establishing a framework for assessment

Within the field of special education, a model of assessment known as assessment-through-teaching has been a widely advocated alternative to norm-referenced approaches. It has been adopted in the area of special needs by teachers and psychologists who have investigated children's learning through classroom-based teaching interventions, and it sees assessment as closely related to the teaching and learning processes. Its applications are potentially much broader, given the advent of teacher assessment and the requirement that schools offer annual reports on children's progress.

The model of assessment-through-teaching (ATT: see Figure 4.2) was first developed by Robert Glaser in 1962. It represents an attempt to show a relationship between

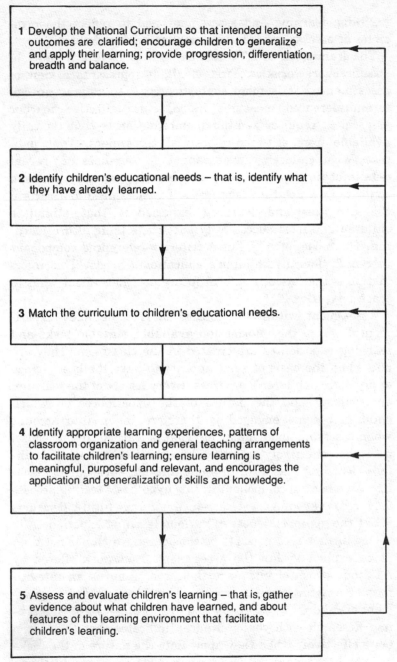

1 Develop the National Curriculum so that intended learning outcomes are clarified; encourage children to generalize and apply their learning; provide progression, differentiation, breadth and balance.

2 Identify children's educational needs – that is, identify what they have already learned.

3 Match the curriculum to children's educational needs.

4 Identify appropriate learning experiences, patterns of classroom organization and general teaching arrangements to facilitate children's learning; ensure learning is meaningful, purposeful and relevant, and encourages the application and generalization of skills and knowledge.

5 Assess and evaluate children's learning – that is, gather evidence about what children have learned, and about features of the learning environment that facilitate children's learning.

Figure 4.2 Assessment-through-teaching

teaching, learning and assessment and to reflect the principles of assessment identified earlier in this chapter.

The framework of ATT can be seen to have a number of specific characteristics. First of all, it represents a view of assessment that is more sophisticated than relying on criterion-referenced measures alone, since effective teacher assessment requires additional information to that typically available from criterion-referenced assessment. That indicates what children can or cannot do, but does not reveal details of how quickly they are learning or the classroom contexts in which they learn best. Teachers need to ascertain the activities and learning experiences that stimulate children and most successfully encourage their future learning. The model of ATT has a criterion-referenced component in Box 2, 'Identify children's educational needs'. This information is then used to inform future decisions about what to teach next (Box 3).

Assessment within the context of ATT becomes 'experimental'. From the information available, suitable tasks and learning experiences are created in the classroom. They are offered on the basis of what appears to have the best chance of promoting children's progress. Every aspect of the learning environment and the nature of the experiences on which children become engaged is therefore taken into account when assessing and evaluating what is learned. In one sense, a teacher effectively creates a hypothesis about what facilitates learning and tests this out through subsequent teaching. An essential component in this hypothesis-testing process is a record-keeping system which informs future decisions about the appropriateness of various learning experiences.

One further area needs to be considered which has not been made explicit within the assessment framework offered by ATT but which should nevertheless be seen as an integral part of any assessment process. This concerns the involvement of children in assessing and evaluating their own learning. Research with young children indicates that they learn more effectively when they appreciate the nature of the tasks on which they are to become engaged. They are likely to learn more effectively through becoming involved in the teaching and learning processes, through negotiating aspects of their learning, through making decisions about the nature of the learning environment and through becoming active partners in assessing and evaluating the outcomes of their efforts.

The information from ATT includes the following:

- what children have and have not learned;
- children's progress in relation to the learning environment;
- the provision required to facilitate learning, particularly in terms of time and resources;
- the circumstances under which children learn best;
- information upon which to make daily decisions in the classroom;
- and from the repeated administration of the criterion-referenced part of assessment, teachers know whether:
  - children transfer their learning from familiar to unfamiliar tasks and activities;
  - learning earlier skills facilitates learning of later skills;
- children's perceptions of their own progress.

Such information enables teachers to focus their attention on children's existing achievements and the classroom circumstances that may facilitate future learning.

The model of ATT effectively brings together mainstream and special education. Until now this model has only emerged in the literature on special education. When teachers have been asked to adopt it, there has been a perception that they are being urged to do something different for a small group of children. This was illustrated in the research conducted by Gipps *et al.* (1987), referred to in Chapter 3, into LEA provision for children with special needs. The current demands on teachers necessitate their engagement in more detailed formal assessments of all the children in a class on a wider basis than has hitherto been the case.

If teachers meet a range of educational needs through adopting similar teaching and assessment approaches for all children, they will be bridging a gap between mainstream and current perceptions of special education. This view that 'good teaching' and 'good special needs teaching' are the same thing was endorsed in Circular 5 from the NCC which stated 'Schools that successfully meet the demands of a diverse range of individual needs through agreed policies on teaching and learning approaches are invariably effective in meeting special educational needs' (NCC, 1989a). This view was endorsed by the observations of HMI (DES, 1989b) in their survey of pupils with special needs in ordinary school, discussed in Chapter 3.

There is, though, one major difficulty that has been experienced in introducing ATT into schools. The initial focus may be on assessment, but this ultimately leads to more general questions being raised about how to teach. Questions about assessment very soon become questions about managing children's learning.

Effective teacher assessment yields continuous data on children's achievements. Studies on the nature of children's learning experiences from educational researchers, and, more informally, HMI observations, have tended to suggest that the level of match achieved by teachers in the work they offer children in relation to their existing achievements is rarely as high as might be considered desirable. In other words, regular assessments revealed that many children were on inappropriate tasks. For example, the research by Bennett *et al.* (1984) showed that teachers concentrated largely on introducing new material and practice tasks, and were not helping children to apply their knowledge, which is what they claimed to be doing.

ATT also requires that teachers critically evaluate the quality of their own teaching and recognize that many learning problems arise from factors existing within the school. However, Croll and Moses' (1985) examination of teachers' views on the causes behind pupils' difficulties in schools indicated that there was a clear reluctance to attribute difficulties to factors lying within the school. The main reason for a child being either a 'slow learner' or a 'poor reader' was attributed to the child's 'IQ/ability', or 'other within-child factors' or 'home/parent'. In less than 3 per cent of cases were difficulties related to school/teacher factors. The 428 teachers in the study were reluctant to accept responsibility for children failing to learn.

One conclusion which can be drawn from the above research is that the more we assess, the more we find out about the effectiveness of teaching and learning. This may prove uncomfortable when we discover that a child is not learning. ATT requires a willingness to see a failure to make satisfactory progress as a problem which can be resolved through examining and amending the learning environment. This includes the curriculum, the range of learning experiences offered to children, patterns of classroom organization, the teaching approaches adopted to facilitate progress and children's perceptions of their learning. Judging by the finding of Croll and Moses, teachers appear reluctant to adopt this position as their staring point.

To summarize, therefore, National Curriculum assessment requires teachers to gather detailed evidence on children's learning. The advice offered to teachers in official publications and recent research implies that learning outcomes should be articulated in relation to the observable. Many teachers in special education have extensive experience in this area, and are aware that a naive collection of behavioural evidence does not necessarily demonstrate children's learning. The past experiences of those in special education can help teachers to develop a framework for describing children's learning and to relate this to a process of assessment for all children. The areas of learning to be promoted by teachers, identified earlier, imply a curriculum which is broad and balanced, and encourages children to generalize and apply their knowledge, skills and concepts.

Precision teaching

Precision teaching is an approach to assessment that has been widely used in special education. Its name has often been found to be misleading, since it is not actually a method of teaching but a way of finding out whether children are learning and bridging the gap that exists between their attainments and those of their peers. Through regular assessment, teachers find out whether selected teaching methods are effective. Successful methods are retained and unsuccessful ones are revised, and their subsequent effects systematically reviewed. Thus the effectiveness of teaching is under regular scrutiny, with methods being adapted when necessary to promote children's learning.

Precision teaching emphasizes the need for carefully structured curricula, provides techniques for collecting detailed information on children's progress and enables teachers to evaluate the effectiveness of selected teaching procedures. Precision teaching does not provide details about how to teach but informs teachers as to whether chosen methods have been successful.

There are five basic steps in precision teaching. The first specifies desired learning outcomes in observable terms. Subsequent steps require that children's progress is recorded daily, is expressed visually on specially prepared charts and is related to the teaching methods adopted by the teacher. Finally, overall progress is evaluated daily to determine whether it is satisfactory or whether changes are required to accelerate progress still more, to help bridge the curriculum gap that exists between children and their peers.

The potential appeal of precision teaching as an approach to assessment is that it does not initially require teachers to adopt particular styles of teaching or to use particular resources. Ideally teachers use methods which they believe to be most successful, and which reflect existing practice and their own values and beliefs about learning and teaching. The principles and techniques of precision teaching are then used to assess the effectiveness of the teachers' own preferred methods. The aim is to help teachers become effective problem-solvers in the classroom. They create their own hypotheses about why children's progress is not satisfactory, take steps to overcome any problems and then evaluate the outcomes of their interventions.

Precision teaching potentially plays a key role in enabling

teachers to gather detailed evidence on the progress of children experiencing difficulties on a day-to-day basis. The principles of precision teaching can also be applied directly to the Key Stage teacher assessments of all the children in a class, not only those experiencing problems. The next section therefore considers some general issues about standard assessment tasks (SATs) before exploring their implications for children with learning difficulties.

Standard assessment tasks

Teacher assessments are to be augmented when children are 7, 11, 14 and 16 by the Key Stage assessments made through administering SATs. Since these were first introduced, the government has claimed that the Key Stage assessments are essential to giving parents information about the respective merits of different schools. The assumption underlying this belief is that comparisons can be readily made and that parents will then be likely to move their children from the less to the more successful schools.

In the past, when progress was determined through norm-referenced assessment it was often felt that children did not perform to a level which reflected their true competence, because they were intimidated or overawed by the unfamiliar nature of the 'testing procedures', SATs were designed to overcome these problems. Initially, therefore, the Key Stage assessments involved giving children of the same age the same tasks, which mirrored everyday school activities. However, the resulting SATs were found to be extremely demanding on time and resources and were subject to considerable criticism. As a result, they have subsequently been revised and streamlined, and are moving steadily towards being a series of paper-and-pencil activities, which increasingly resemble the old 11-plus in style if not actual content.

One consequence of these amendments and revisions is that the SATs no longer reflect typical classroom activities and so are less likely to yield reliable and valid results. However, as schools are under increasing pressure to revert to what are termed 'formal' teaching methods, it may well be that the new SATs will no longer be so unfamiliar, in form or content, to future generations of schoolchildren.

The Key Stage assessments can be seen to be both criterion-referenced and normative. It is argued that they help parents to see what their children have learned, and in this sense they are criterion-referenced. They are also designed so that comparisons can be made between children in different schools and in different parts of the country, and this represents the normative dimension to assessment. However, it is debatable whether the Key Stage assessments can fulfil either of these aims.

Can the reporting of children's results on the SATs indicate what they have learned? Within very broad parameters, possibly. But each level covers a number of attainment targets and such wide areas of learning that it is hardly meaningful to state that a child has attained level 2 in English and maths and level 3 in science.

The SATs are supposed to indicate what children have learned, but provide no indication of progress over time. This makes comparisons about schools' relative effectiveness difficult. A group of 7-year-olds who are all at level 3 in mathematics might have achieved this stage as 6-year-olds and made little progress over the last twelve months. Similarly, a comparison of two schools based on SATs may indicate that they have performed equally well; however, when children's previous knowledge is taken into account, it may become clear that children at one school have learned far more than those at the other. It is therefore difficult to make meaningful decisions about relative effectiveness until it is known what skills, knowledge and concepts children had already learned when they entered school. What also needs to be remembered in relation to a school's effectiveness is that we know they have strengths and weaknesses which are not necessarily reflected in the SATs. Judging a school's qualities is a finely balanced process which involves looking at the whole school, taking into account a variety of factors and ultimately relating these to the needs of individual children.

The introduction of the Key Stage assessments has a

number of potential implications for children seen to have difficulties. To report a single level of achievement for children, as discussed, does not reflect the degree of learning which may well have occurred. A child may be reported as being at level 1 in English, but this may not do justice to the learning which has taken place. Schools which in the past had made a commitment to children with special needs may be forced to rethink their position. First, children with difficulties will probably do less well on the SATs and this will be reflected in the school's overall results. Secondly, parents may believe that children with difficulties will make excessively high demands on teacher time in the classroom, and that their children will be neglected.

Paradoxically, though, the more the SATs take the form of paper-and-pencil tests, the more highly will curriculum-based teacher assessment come to be valued by parents. It will only be the teacher assessment that can then give the details of overall progress and convey a realistic impression of children's improvements over time. It is these detailed assessments and the knowledge and understanding that they can offer that have a crucial role to play in both the day-to-day interchanges between teachers, children and parents, and the statutory assessment procedure associated with the 1981 Education Act.

The statutory assessment procedure

This is the process of identifying a child's educational needs and the most appropriate provision to meet those needs under the requirements of the 1981 Education Act. The procedure can be initiated by anyone who has reasonable grounds for supposing that a child has special educational needs. In reality, the person is most likely to be a child's teacher or parents. The person does so by notifying the director of education, who then contacts the relevant personnel to request a written report (known as their 'advice') on whether the child in question has special educational needs.

Parents are formally notified that an assessment period is about to start to ascertain their child's educational needs and that they can make their own views known to representatives of the LEA. Once parental permission has been given, the director of education asks a child's teachers, an educational psychologist and the school medical officer for their professional opinions about the child's educational needs.

Each professional then undertakes a period of assessment of the child's needs. It is desirable, and likely in the majority of cases, that teachers and psychologists will already have consulted and collaborated in depth before initiating the statutory assessment procedure. Similarly, it is to be hoped that parents will have been fully involved in any school-based work already undertaken to establish a child's educational needs. The statutory assessment, under these circumstances, is a largely administrative task, in which information has already been collected over time following a period of assessment-through-teaching. Under such circumstances the process can be completed well within the time scale recommended by the Audit Commission (1992).

Unfortunately, the statutory assessment is not always preceded by a detailed teacher assessment. This may be because a child has recently moved to a school and teachers identify previously unrecognized problems, or because parents feel their child is experiencing difficulties and notify the director of education directly. It is preferable that teachers and psychologists base their opinions on information gathered over time, but sometimes for practical or ideological reasons normatively based assessments are preferred to the criterion-referenced or ipsative alternatives.

Teachers, educational psychologists and school medical officers write reports known as the advice, and are required to comment from their own particular perspective on children's educational needs and on the provision to meet them. Each professional is responsible for his or her own advice and so must feel confident that the opinions offered can be substantiated and give an accurate account of his or her understanding of the child's needs. All professionals can present their advice in the way they feel best, as no guidance is available on this matter from government sources.

Once all the advice has been received, it is then up to the designated LEA officer acting on behalf of the director of education to determine whether special educational provision is necessary to meet the child's educational needs. The various professionals offer their own views on the child's needs based on their assessments, but they advise rather than make a decision; and it is in the nature of 'advice' that it can be accepted or rejected by the LEA.

Where advice from the professionals conflicts, the LEA may well arrange a meeting to try to resolve differing perceptions. In these circumstances, it is particularly important to substantiate opinion with appropriate assessment data, collected over time, which illustrates what a child has been able to achieve with existing resources and school provision. Continuous assessment over a long period will be valued more than information from a single occasion.

Ultimately a decision has to be made by the LEA about the child's educational needs. If a statement is issued, it goes to parents in draft form first. They then have an opportunity to comment on its contents. Interestingly, the professionals contributing advice do not receive a draft copy, are not invited to comment on the LEA's decisions and have no formal opportunity to draw attention to places where their advice has been either ignored or misinterpreted. It is therefore important that parents liaise fully with teachers, psychologists and any other independent professional when reviewing the draft statement. The issues raised by the statementing procedure and parents' responses to them are explored more fully in Chapter 6.

This chapter has introduced different approaches to assessment and considered them in relation to the aims and practicalities of effective teacher assessment. The 1988 Education Act requires teachers to monitor children's learning systematically so that parents can receive annual reports on their progress. Approaches to assessment adopted in special education have specific relevance in assisting teachers in this role. Lessons learned in the past should ensure that children learn to generalize and apply their learning in a wide range of meaningful contexts. Ultimately, though, despite the pressures being placed on schools to be accountable, the aim of the approaches to assessment described in this chapter is to help teachers understand how children are learning in their classroom, so that they can collaborate with parents and children in making learning an enjoyable and successful experience for all concerned.

Chapter 5

UNDERSTANDING AND MANAGING CHILDREN'S BEHAVIOUR

Introduction

In any classroom or group setting, teachers will at some time have children whose behaviour poses a problem. However, perceptions of troublesome behaviour vary from teacher to teacher. What one teacher finds unacceptable another may not, and vice versa. So when dealing with the notion of children with behaviour problems, it is always within the context of the perceptions, attitudes and values of teachers.

This chapter takes a broad overview of the range of factors that underpin teachers' perceptions of disruptive or unwelcome behaviour. It explores:

- the nature of classroom behaviour;
- the influence of family background on children's behaviour;
- its implications for teachers;
- the ways teachers can respond to and promote children's social development.

The chapter concludes with an examination of how to manage children's unwanted behaviour.

When thinking about troublesome behaviour, it is helpful to take as a starting point our own experiences as pupils in schools, particularly secondary schools. It is in secondary schools that children come into contact with as many as seven or eight teachers every day. The standard of behaviour displayed by children varies with each teacher. As a class group, children very quickly find out what teachers will allow and what behaviour is unwelcome. Children can be perfectly behaved one minute but resurface as a far more troublesome proposition only minutes later, in a new lesson with a different teacher. What factors give rise to such sudden transformations in behaviour?

The nature of classroom behaviour

Children's classroom behaviour does not exist in a vacuum and should therefore be considered in relation to the various school-related factors which influence its development. We know ourselves that our own behaviour is affected by the context in which it occurs. The way we behave at home with out families is different from our behaviour in other social or work contexts. Thus, behaviour varies with social contexts, with different friends and even with the same friend, our behaviour can change depending on circumstances and our mood. We are capable of a wide spectrum of behaviour, and the same is true of children.

It is unwise to make categorical statements about particular children. If their behaviour is unacceptable to us, it cannot be assumed that they behave in the same way with other adults or teachers. Nevertheless, when we find their behaviour irksome and unwanted, with negative effects on peers, the natural tendency is to state that children are 'disruptive' or 'have emotional and behaviour problems'. However, there are difficulties associated with these descriptions. They suggest that we are referring to a 'condition' which children have, and this carries implications for our understanding of its causes and treatment. Furthermore, they implicitly and potentially pre-empt any debate about the classroom or school environments as possible influences on the child's behaviour. If we are trying to identify a condition or disorder, we may be tempted to assess children in isolation, without reference to the contexts in which their behaviour occurs.

Ironically the use of labels (such as 'disruptive', 'aggressive', 'disobedient', etc.) can be seen as conveying more information about the teachers using the terms than the individuals to whom they are applied. This issue was also discussed in Chapter 3. The description we offer of children represents a personal statement about ourselves.

Referring to a child as 'disruptive' can be seen as a short-hand way of expressing a judgement about the child's behaviour. It reflects the fact that our observations of behaviour lead to conclusions about the child's motives and intent. It does not indicate the type of behaviour that is being displayed, its frequency, its impact on others or the circumstances under which it occurs. In using the term 'disruptive', a comment is being passed about the child.

Since our interpretations of other people's behaviour are essentially personal, they are likely to be coloured by our own expectations and values. Thus, teachers may react differently to the same behaviour by a pupil depending on the way they see it and on their expectations. One may read a child's smile when reprimanded as 'insolent'; another may suppose that it is a 'nervous' response or sign of embarrassment. These different personal views may result in quite dissimilar ways of handling the same situation.

Subjective interpretations of behaviour also tend to be vague and open to problems of miscommunication; for example, the blanket terms 'disruptive' or 'aggressive'. We could assume that these words mean the same to everyone. However, different behaviour could be covered by the term 'disruptive'. Does the teacher mean the child was humming, talking out of turn, throwing paper darts, knocking over chairs, or perhaps some other activity? The teacher may mean that the child behaved in one way on Monday and in another way on Tuesday. A colleague's or parent's understanding of the word disruptive may not match the behaviour it was intended to describe. The use of labels is confusing and unhelpful. It gives an impression that presented problems can be overcome by focusing any intervention approaches exclusively on the child in question rather than on the environment.

So far, the discussion has focused on classroom behaviour and suggested that this should be the centre of attention in attempting to resolve difficulties. However, seeing children's behaviour as troublesome is a personal matter for teachers. It is, therefore, important to understand why teachers feel there is a problem and how it can be overcome. Although there are other factors, particularly the home environment, which have an impact on children's social development and school behaviour, teachers have neither the time nor the expertise to initiate prolonged investigations into children's family life. What they can influence is children's behaviour in the classroom, irrespective of the child's other circumstances and behaviour at home. We are all capable of displaying different behaviour in different settings. Nevertheless, it is helpful to illustrate the potential impact of children's home environment on their school behaviour and to consider its implications for teachers.

The influence of family background

In what ways might teachers expect family life to influence the behaviour of children in their classrooms? Very little extensive research has been carried out in this area in the United Kingdom, and although it might be possible to predict which children are more likely to be viewed as problematical in schools, such predictions are likely to be stereotypical and to create a self-fulfilling prophecy. However, there are some areas of family background that may impinge on a child's classroom behaviour but have received little attention.

Children grow up in a variety of environments. Many are raised in homes by one or two parents, or by a natural parent and a step-parent, and yet others may be taken into the care of local authorities. Children's understanding of what is acceptable and unacceptable behaviour is a reflection of their previous environments and the overt and covert messages they convey.

In the early years of life children can be seen as active sense-makers, striving to understand the patterns of behaviour they observe around them. They will see their parents (or other primary caretakers) interacting with each other and will draw conclusions about their own interaction and relationships. The presence or absence of siblings also has a significant bearing on life experiences.

During the first couple of years, for the majority of children, the mother is the most significant person in their lives. She is responsible for feeding and providing for their immediate needs. As children grow older, fathers feature more prominently in their world. Fathers have a significant role to play in helping children to appreciate how the wider social world functions.

Newborn babies are dependent on their parents for everything. When they cry, parents almost invariably respond immediately, which conveys to children a sense of omnipotence – a feeling which, if it persists, is far from positive. Life cannot always revolve round children in this way and it is up to parents to help them realize their limited power over others. As children grow older, they try to work out their relationships with significant people in their lives. They need to recognize that others also have desires, needs and preferences, which may compete with their own but are equally valid. This process has been referred to by Robin Skynner and John Cleese, in their widely read book *Families and How to Survive Them* (Methuen, London, 1984), as 'getting on your own map'. 'Being on your own map' implies a recognition that others have opinions and rights that, when they conflict with yours, can best be resolved through discussion and negotiation. One of the responsibilities of parents is to help children learn socially acceptable forms of behaviour and to 'get on their own map'.

Parents enable children to adopt a more realistic view of life through laying down some rules and outlining the boundaries of acceptable social behaviour. Recognizing that you cannot have everything your own way is a painful but essential lesson to learn. However, what happens if children come to school and have never learned this? Let us suppose their parents always give into them at the merest hint of a tantrum. It may come as quite a shock to such children, on arrival at school, to find that they cannot do just as they like, that there are social conventions to be followed, and that the needs of other children have to be considered as well as their own.

Young children are constantly engaged in a process of hypothesis-testing in their attempts to understand their surroundings. The clearer the patterns of parental behaviour appear, the more likely children are to appreciate the significance of what is happening and to recognize that much of our behaviour is governed by subtle but well-established social rules and rituals. Children develop their understandings of the world from these family-oriented observations, and it is helpful for teachers to recognize the origins of children's unique understanding of the world. Establishing appropriate patterns of behaviour early in a child's experiences helps them to begin to make sense of life. Ultimately, parents' responses to their children and to each other have direct implications for teachers.

When children begin school, they are entering a whole new world. The patterns of behaviour which were acceptable at home may not be accepted at school. Movement around the classroom is sometimes restricted; children cannot eat just when they like; they can only go outside with the prior approval of the teacher. Instead of either having the sole attention of one adult or sharing that adult with three or four children, a child has to compete with twenty or thirty others for the teacher's time. Life is less predictable than it was. Previous constructions of the world have to be put to the test and may need revising. Think how we, as adults, respond to a new job or changes in our personal circumstances. We are likely to experience some degree of stress when we make changes in our lives. Imagine, then, the demands being made on 4- or 5-year-olds as they proceed in their new world.

In these new school contexts, children set out to try to establish the ground rules for their behaviour. At home, parents indicate the boundaries of what is and is not acceptable behaviour. Children will have similar expectations that their teacher will also provide a framework for their behaviour. This may emerge through discussion or be deduced through classroom interactions early on in the new school year. Once aware of the boundaries, children will proceed to 'test them out', to establish whether they will be enforced by the teacher,

Children first engage in this process of testing out boundaries, to the continued chagrin of their parents, around the age of 2, at the stage known as the 'terrible twos'. At this age, children begin to learn that their needs cannot or will not be satisfied immediately by parents as they were when they were younger. However, children do not willingly accept these new constraints on their actions without assessing whether their parents will enforce the new boundaries. So children resist their parents and defy their wishes. They have the major 'temper tantrums' that characterize the terrible twos, and which are often focused on the refusal by a harassed parent to buy the chocolates and sweets so attractively displayed at the supermarket checkout counter.

The encounter turns into a battle of willpower, whose outcome has considerable implications for teachers. If the parents recognize that this stage of development is an essential milestone for children to reach, they will be helping their children to appreciate that they cannot always have just what they want, and those children will have a more realistic view of their position in the real world. Where this does not happen, children may learn that they can get their own way through their temper tantrums.

Some children arrive at school never having learned that they cannot have their own way, that they are part of a larger social network, that there are others who have needs, and that they have to take their turn in receiving adult attention. Others will appreciate that there are social rules which govern their interactions and that there are limits to what is generally acceptable social behaviour.

The implications for teachers is that from time to time they may well find themselves teaching children who have not learned the usual social conventions. Such children may believe that a fearsome display of temper will get them their own way at school just as it invariably does at home. Here the teacher is faced with the task of facilitating the children's social development and providing them with a suitable framework for their social interactions.

Ideally this task would be undertaken in conjunction with parents, but this in itself may be problematic. Children will not willingly change their behaviour, especially where it has generally enabled them to function successfully and to get their own way. If in the past parents have been unable to establish guide-lines with their children, it may be more difficult when children are of school age and their behaviour is even more firmly established. Equally, teachers may find that parents are comfortable with their children's behaviour and that there may be a difference between parental and teacher expectations. However, teachers are still faced with the difficulty of managing the children's problematic classroom behaviour.

To summarize, therefore, the impact of family life can contribute to the development of behaviour problems in two ways. The first is that children may still feel that what they say goes and may not appreciate that there are others whose needs have to be accommodated within the classroom. The second is that children learn to adhere to identified social rules, but that parental and teacher expectations may differ so that a child's behaviour is found to be unacceptable by the teacher.

The above discussion illustrates some of the family scenarios and their impact on children's perceptions of school. Overall, family life influences children's perceptions of themselves and others in a profound way. So how children come to think and feel about themselves, how they see themselves in relation to others, their perception of gender roles and ethnic differences all potentially have a bearing on classroom dynamics and social relationships within the school.

Teachers cannot delve into every aspect of children's family lives and determine its influence on their classroom behaviour. In the main, when things are running smoothly, teachers would not do so. When there are problems in school, it is easy to blame family circumstances. There are three reasons why this should be avoided. Firstly, just as family life has had an influence on the child, so teachers' own upbringings influence them. It would be naive to imagine that teachers remain immune from family factors and personal histories influencing their perceptions and behaviour in the classroom. While it is not within the scope of this book to explore these factors, their existence needs to be acknowledged and their impact on teachers' understanding of children's classroom behaviour appreciated. Secondly, the school and learning environments contribute to children's behaviour in the classroom. Thirdly, children learn to behave differently in different contexts. Children can change their behaviour when encouraged to do so.

So far this chapter has discussed the nature of classroom behaviour, and considered how it is influenced by a child's family background. It concludes by discussing the steps that can be taken to prevent and to respond to unwanted classroom behaviour.

Managing classroom behaviour

A preventive approach is naturally preferable to a crisis-oriented one. To develop preventive strategies requires time, planning and commitment. A popular belief about the management of children's behaviour is that it is a natural talent. The Elton Committee in its conclusions attempted to challenge this common assumption, stating:

> A more common belief is that group management skills are simply a natural gift. You either have it or you don't. Our evidence does not support this belief. Its most damaging feature is that teachers who have difficulty controlling classes tend to put this down to personal inadequacy rather than to a lack of particular skills which can be acquired through training or advice from colleagues. (DES, 1989a, para. 3.13)

In identifying the skills mentioned by the Elton Committee, it is helpful to see the classroom environment as comprising three components:

- the physical component;
- the educational component;
- the social component.

The physical component. This refers to the actual layout of the classroom and the available non-curricular resources. They are those aspects of the classroom which can be planned and organized without the children being present. So this includes seating arrangements and location of resources which can be determined by teachers, as well as those other factors over which they have less control, such as lighting and heating.

The educational component. This derives from the content of the school's curricula. The learning experiences children are offered and the patterning of activities across the school day are all key features of the educational component, and are discussed in more detail in Chapters 3 and 4. Children's behaviour cannot be divorced from the nature of their learning experiences. Unwanted behaviour is more likely when learning opportunities are neither stimulating nor geared to children's educational needs. Various research studies have illustrated that misbehaviour is increasingly evident when work is too difficult and insufficient help is available. Suggestions which come later in this chapter on managing unwanted behaviour are presented on the assumption that the education component will be reviewed.

The social component. This refers to the way in which teachers and children interact, and provides the focus for the remainder of this chapter. The major concern of many new teachers and students is how to get control of a class. Perhaps it is this concern that, paradoxically, serves to undermine teachers' management of children's classroom behaviour, because *they do not have to get control – they already have it.* Their status as teachers ensures that they are initially in control. Unfortunately what they can do is *lose* control, a position from which it is often hard to recover.

Behaving like a teacher and conveying enthusiasm

The starting point for effective behaviour management is to behave like a teacher and convey the status consistent with occupying that role, rather than wrestle with the problem of getting control. Despite frequent adverse publicity, teachers are generally seen to be have status, particularly with younger children. Older pupils too start out with the expectation that the person standing in front of them will perform certain functions in his or her role as teacher. Unwanted behaviour is more likely to occur when teachers behave in a manner which undermines and belies their status and role. The behaviour that would be displayed by a teacher trying to get control of a class would not be compatible with demonstrating that you already had control.

Status can therefore be seen to be conveyed in at least two ways. The first is through a teacher's general manner in the classroom, and the second is through the way learning experiences are organized and implemented within the school day. Teachers who are confident, enthusiastic and already in control will communicate this to children, not only through what they say but also through their general demeanour. Children in the early stages of contact with a new teacher observe carefully, and although they will be attending to what is said, it will be the wider, non-verbal elements in their interactions that reinforce or undermine the teacher's position in the classroom.

Non-verbal behaviour

The importance of a teacher's non-verbal behaviour has become increasingly appreciated in recent years and is one area in education that can be supported by a large body of research. The key areas of non-verbal behaviour are:

- posture;
- eye contact;
- gesture;
- dress;
- movement and use of space.

Effective teachers and communicators use their posture, eye contact, gestures and dress to enhance the verbal content of any interaction. Their posture indicates interest and enthusiasm, eye contact is willingly established and maintained, gestures are firm and decisive and the clothes worn are consistent with having status.

Through their movement round the classroom and their use of space, teachers demonstrate their status and willingness to behave like teachers. Teachers can and should move round the classroom freely during activities. As children at school, we may have come across teachers who were able to convey the impression that they had eyes in the back of their heads – they could spot incidents even when their backs were turned. Teachers achieve this by moving round the classroom, varying their position and constantly scanning the room to monitor children's behaviour and activities.

Through regular movement, teachers are less predictable. The children do not know where they will be and so cannot find a comfortable position where they can hide away and avoid work. Frequent movement also indicates to children that teachers are exercising the right they have as high-status people to move around the classroom. Children's movements are regulated by teachers. A failure to move around the classroom, particularly at the primary level, is potentially suggesting to children that the teacher does not have the confidence or inclination to do so, and consequently is less likely to be seen to be behaving in a manner consistent with being a 'good teacher'.

Sometimes teachers sit at their desks with a line of children waiting to have work marked. It is difficult to monitor children's activities from this position, especially when the children around the desk shield their peers from the teacher's direct vision. Again, one potentially negative message to children suggests that the teacher is 'hiding' and will not come out from behind her or his desk, or is for some reason unwilling to do so.

The final point to be made in this section on non-verbal behaviour concerns the interpersonal distance between teachers and pupils. In all our social interactions we operate as if we were cocooned in our own private bubble. We maintain a certain distance, determined by the nature of the interaction and the person with whom we are interacting. Teachers, however, are able to invade the personal space of children, and children will regard this as quite legitimate. Children will permit their teachers to move close to them, to pick up their work or removed any objects which prove to be a distraction.

It is now well known that politicians have employed consultants to advise on non-verbal aspects of their behaviour, so as to communicate as convincingly as possible. Teaching is also about communicating effectively, as well as stimulating children's interest in classroom activities. Effective use of posture, eye contact, gesture and dress are part of this process. They are fundamental to the management of children's behaviour and need attention and practice.

Teacher expectations for children's behaviour

What teachers expect to happen in the classroom has a significant bearing on ensuing events. They usually have clear expectations which reflect attitudes and values for children's personal qualities and the nature of their classroom behaviour. Teacher expectations encompass the ways the daily business of classroom life should be conducted; for example, how children should attract teacher attention, move around the classroom, sharpen pencils, etc. Within the range of expected behaviour, it is possible to identify and prioritize acceptable behaviour. These expectations effectively comprise a 'behavioural curriculum'. It may be unusual to think in this way, because it is assumed that children already know how to behave appropriately. But as teacher expectations vary so widely, it is necessary to clarify codes of behaviour on initial contact with a new class.

Communicating teacher expectations

In earlier sections in this chapter, the importance of parents' defining the parameters of behaviour to children was discussed. Individual teachers also need to make their expectations known to children. Within the school context, these expectations are often expressed as rules, but it might be more helpful to think of them as guide-lines.

These guide-lines can be developed through discussion and negotiation with the children. They make teacher expectations more explicit, so that they are presented to children directly rather than being left for them to deduce on their own through trial and error. Children will attempt to ascertain the parameters for their behaviour even if they are not introduced by the teacher. It is, therefore, not a question of whether or not to present children with guide-lines but of how this is to be done.

Often guide-lines are presented in a negative way. They state what children should not do (for example, 'Don't run in the classroom'). This does not inform children how they *should* conduct themselves in the classroom. The more positive way of communicating expectations indicates what they *are* expected to do (for example, 'Put up your hand if you want attention').

Most teachers inevitably prefer an ordered classroom where children are well disposed to following out daily activities purposefully and with a minimum of disruption. Yet few teachers, if any, will teach a class without unwanted behaviour occurring from time to time. In part this can be attributed to the social dynamics of the classroom, where children try to find out whether teachers are willing to enforce guide-lines, and to recognize the boundaries of acceptable behaviour. How teachers respond during this testing-out phase often establishes patterns of behaviour for the remainder of the school year.

Testing the guide-lines. What needs to be remembered and anticipated, therefore, is that when children are presented with new guide-lines it is likely that they will:

- test out the extent to which the new frameworks will be adhered to by the teacher. This is almost inevitable even if they have been negotiated, discussed and agreed with the pupils beforehand. It reveals the teacher's resolve in implementing the new guide-lines;
- resist, before changing their behaviour. Potential changes are a source of stress and it is far more comfortable to stay the same.

Responding to children's behaviour

Organizing the three components of the classroom environment (physical, educational and social) is the basis for interactions between teachers and pupils. At the beginning of a new year children assess their new teacher, observing how the teacher relates to them, how their behaviour is managed, how the teacher encourages or reprimands, the activities they are asked to undertake and how the teacher responds to their success and problems in learning.

The start of the school year is an anxious time for many children, as they leave their familiar setting with a previous teacher and start the learning process all over again with someone new. It is equally likely that a new teacher will also be somewhat anxious at the beginning of the year; or on first contact with a new group of children, although for possibly different reasons.

Given this scenario, the more welcoming the teacher is during these early stages the better. Teachers need to be positive about acceptable behaviour, even if it is not exceptional or would not justify comment at other times in the school year. Recent research suggests that teachers are more likely to express disapproval than approval of children's behaviour. Since certain patterns of behaviour are expected, it is often felt that they do not, therefore, deserve comment or praise. However, some children benefit greatly from receiving praise and reminders of what is acceptable.

Commenting on expected behaviour also performs one further essential function: it is a key element in the much more important process of helping children to take responsibility for their own behaviour. Providing children with feedback helps them to become more aware of their own behaviour and to make links between their actions and its consequences. Learning that certain actions have certain effects enables children to progress towards monitoring, regulating and being responsible for their own behaviour.

Being consistent

Earlier discussion in this chapter considered the way children interpret the world around them and strive to make sense of life. Similarly, in the classroom teachers need to be consistent from day to day and week to week in their overall management of children's behaviour. Clearly, if children receive praise one week and criticism the next for doing exactly the same thing, they are likely to become confused about what is acceptable. If the same behaviour from two children is responded to differently (positively in the case of one child and negatively in that of the other), this potentially gives rise to confusion, and possibly resentment as well, on the part of the class. Where consistency can be achieved, teachers are seen to be fair, which helps to enlist the children's support and trust. Clear messages help children to appreciate that it is specific forms of behaviour which are praised, rather than some children being held up as examples of being 'good' pupils.

Modelling

Teachers have authority and status within the classroom. They have a responsibility to behave towards the children in ways that are consistent with their position and the behaviour they are encouraging. In the previous section the importance of teachers behaving consistently towards children over time was highlighted. To this it should be added that their own behaviour and actions should be consistent with the personal qualities being promoted.

Understanding unwanted behaviour

When children behave inappropriately it is helpful to try to gain the appreciation of how they perceive school and teachers. The psychologist George Kelly suggested that each individual has a unique view of the world which is influenced by family and life experiences. He proposed that individual perceptions are shaped through formulating, and then testing out, hypotheses about the nature of social interactions. Successful social relationships are based in part on being able to predict outcomes within a social context. Potentially the most stressful social situations are those which are unfamiliar and where we feel less confident in predicting the behaviour of others, such as at a job interview.

This orientation also provides a framework for beginning to respond to unwanted behaviour. When talking about perceptions of the same events, Kelly suggested that it was helpful to recognize that others hold equally valid perceptions of events to your own, even though they may be different. Resolving different perceptions is not a simple matter of saying one is right and the other wrong: it involves recognizing that events are open to more than one interpretation – they can be construed in more than one way. Thus a child's calling out or wandering around the classroom or constantly sharpening a pencil may be interpreted as disruptive and time-wasting by the teacher, but as a request for help by the child, or as one way of avoiding work which is too difficult or uninteresting.

When lessons run smoothly, differences in perceptions between teachers and pupils are not always apparent. However, when a child is seen to misbehave, the invariably distinct and different perceptions of teacher and child have to be reconciled. It is on such occasions that teachers may find it difficult to acknowledge the perceptions of the child as legitimate. If it is accepted that a number of different but equally valid perspectives can be held about everyday classroom interactions, it may help to examine a typical clash of interpretations between teacher and pupil.

It can be argued that to be an effective 'disruptive pupil' is to engage in highly skilled interactions. A child has to anticipate the teacher's behaviour in response to the prevailing circumstances as well as predict how other children will respond to her or his behaviour. There has to be some pay-off for being disruptive, and this might arise from the teacher's and pupils' reactions to what is done. Poor prediction may mean the child has no 'reward' for his or her behaviour.

As discussed earlier, the teacher's descriptions of a child as 'disruptive' may or may not be revealing something about the child. However, they are highlighting aspects of the teacher's own perceptions and reactions. It is possible to rephrase and reconstrue the teacher's observations of the disruptive pupil. Perhaps what the teacher is saying is 'I find this pupil's behaviour to be disruptive in my lesson. She does not carry out my instruction and I find her presence personally threatening. She is not interested in the work I provide.'

A teacher who is open to the possibility that events can be reinterpreted and reconstrued will probably be a different 'kind of teacher' from someone who cannot. To acknowledge that children have a point of view is to open up the potential for negotiation and to recognize the legitimacy of children's perceptions. It is also to see them as people with rights to valid observations of and reactions to classroom life.

This does not mean that unacceptable or unwanted behaviour should be tolerated in the classroom. However, recognizing children's stances and their perceptions provides a basis for dealing with their inappropriate actions. Dealing with unwanted behaviour can be reduced to a set of techniques which can be implemented in response to the identified undesired actions. However, to do so does not acknowledge the significance of the child's and teacher's backgrounds. Both parties come to social interactions with perceptions and expectations for each other's behaviour. Acknowledging these provides a more positive framework and sensitive starting point for considering specific strategies for managing and subsequently reducing unwanted behaviour.

Which behaviour is unwanted?

It will be helpful to indicate the types of behaviour teachers consider unwanted. In 1989 the Elton Committee (DES, 1989a) reported on discipline in schools. The committee commissioned a survey of teachers' views about the nature and frequency of disruptive incidents in school. Over 3,500 teachers responded to the survey (89 per cent of primary teachers and 79 per cent of secondary teachers) drawn from 220 primary and 250 secondary schools. In primary and secondary schools, talking out of turn, hindering other pupils (for example, by distracting them from work, interfering with equipment or materials) and making unnecessary (non-verbal) noise (for instance, by scraping chairs, banging objects, moving clumsily) were reported as occurring most frequently on a daily and weekly basis. Other frequently occurring behaviour reported was: getting out of the seat without permission; calculated idleness or work avoidance; general rowdiness; not being punctual; and persistently infringing class (or school) rules.

Interestingly, one area where differences existed between the primary and secondary sectors was in relation to physical aggression and verbal abuse. In primary schools 74 per cent of teachers reported that pupils were physically aggressive towards other pupils at least once during a week. The figure for secondary schools was 42 per cent. The least frequently reported behaviour was physical destructiveness (for example, breaking objects, damaging furniture and fabric), verbal abuse and physical aggression towards teachers. This was also true of secondary teachers, who reported fewer incidences of physical aggression towards themselves weekly than their primary colleagues.

It may be surprising to some to find that incidences of actual physical aggression by pupils towards both pupils and teachers are fewer in secondary than primary schools.

101

However, teachers within the secondary sector do report increased incidences of general rowdiness, not being punctual, persistent infringement of class and school rules, and cheeky or impertinent remarks or responses compared with their primary colleagues.

A picture sometimes portrayed in the media, and one referred to by the Elton Committee, is that of our schools in a state of rapid decline and frequently at the centre of widespread physical violence. While it would be a mistake to read too much into the findings of the Elton Committee, they do moderate the popular view of what is happening in our schools.

Identifying the frequency of behaviour, however, is only a tip-of-the-iceberg perspective on the nature of classroom interactions. It tells us nothing about the circumstances and contexts under which the reported incidents actually occur. It is only when we begin to delve more deeply that we can begin to appreciate the factors which lead some teachers to view children's behaviour as disruptive and troublesome.

Responding to unwanted behaviour

It is necessary to make a key distinction between the children and the behaviour they display. When we communicate to children that aspects of their behaviour are not acceptable, we need to emphasize that it is the behaviour that is unwanted and unacceptable, not the child. The aim is for children to appreciate that they are still liked and valued, even when their behaviour is the subject of discussion and concern.

The natural inclination of many when observing unwanted behaviour is to criticize the children concerned and tell them not to do it again. However, constant criticism can, paradoxically, help maintain the actual behaviour it is intended to eliminate. Some children would rather have teacher attention, even if it is of a negative, critical nature, than have no attention at all. So they continue to misbehave in order to get attention. This is a phenomenon which has become known as the *criticism trap*.

Criticism tends to lose its impact when overused. Where critical comment becomes the norm, children become desensitized to it. In fact, for criticism to have an impact it has to be offset by more positive interactions – there have to be more positive exchanges than negative ones before criticism leads to a decrease in unwanted behaviour.

Where children are given guide-lines for their behaviour which are supported by positive contact with teachers and where praise is offered frequently but appropriately, there is a range of alternatives to criticism open to teachers for discouraging unwanted behaviour. These alternatives apply to the physical, educational and social environments which can be adapted and amended to decrease the likelihood of unwanted behaviour.

Advice frequently offered for managing unwanted behaviour is to ignore its presence. When unaccompanied by any other response this is unlikely to produce the desired outcomes. Ignoring unwanted behaviour becomes most effective when it is coupled with a more positive response, directing children's attention to more acceptable behaviour and away from the misbehaviour. If a child repeatedly calls out, the teacher might direct the children's attention to another child and say 'Well done, Dean, I'm pleased to see that you've got your hand up. I will come over to help you now.' The teacher is indicating that attention is given for following guide-lines, and not through calling out. Later the child who called out would be told he or she could get help if his or her hand was raised. Adopting this strategy depends on the nature of the unwanted behaviour and its consequences for other pupils. It is clearly not advisable to ignore any actions which place children in any physical danger.

Quite often non-verbal signals are a sufficient response to unwanted behaviour – perhaps eye contact or a gesture which redirects the child's attention back to the task or activity in hand. Low-key responses such as these enable teachers to maintain lesson momentum. They do not need to interrupt the rest of the class and draw attention to the unwanted behaviour. In addition, the teacher is focusing on what is acceptable rather than the alternatives.

Obviously these strategies work best when they rarely interrupt individuals and groups, when teacher attention is minimal and when they are applied in a relaxed, matter-of-fact manner, consistent with high status and good modelling. Responding to unwanted behaviour becomes more stressful when a teacher is uncertain about how best to react to it. Advance planning can help reduce the stress and anxiety associated with classroom disruption.

There may well be occasions when teachers have to deal with behaviour which has consequences that require different strategies to those just summarized. Such behaviour is:

- often more persistent misbehaviour;
- more serious in its effects;
- likely to interrupt a child's own learning or that of peers;
- capable of harming others.

Implementing appropriate strategies is most likely to be successful when:

- children's behaviour can be defined clearly by the teacher so as to avoid inconsistency;
- children fully appreciate why it is unacceptable;
- it is dealt with immediately.

Strategies for dealing with more persistent misbehaviour include:

- removing pleasant events, rather than imposing unpleasant events;
- the child making up for what has been done, such as paying for broken equipment;
- removing children from a potentially volatile situation to another part of the classroom or to another room altogether.

Implementing these measures should be kept to a minimum and needs to be carried out carefully and in a systematic manner. They are most likely to be successful in the context of a classroom where there is frequent teacher praise and approval for children.

Successful behaviour management is geared to preventing major conflicts or dealing with them in a way which causes minimum disruption and allows the lesson to proceed. Where major conflicts develop between teachers and pupils it is unlikely that they can ever be resolved satisfactorily in front of an entire class group. Giving children a way out and a cooling-off period is more likely to be a successful starting point for discussion than a public resolution of the problem.

The steps to be taken in the event of serious and persistent unwanted behaviour are as follows:

Step 1 Examine your own reactions to both the child and her or his behaviour.

Step 2 Pinpoint precisely what the child is doing that causes concern.

Step 3 Observe the unwanted behaviour(s), noting:
- frequency;
- duration;
- the setting in which it occurs (that is, how generalized or situation-specific it is).

Step 4 Relate children's unwanted behaviour to that of their peers in terms of:
- the expected behaviour for children of a similar age in similar circumstances;
- the extent to which unwanted behaviour interrupts or interferes with peers;
- how peers respond.

The information they elicit is helpful when discussing with parents whether or not to involve any support services. The earlier section on the way families influence behaviour outlined one way in which home circumstances are reflected in children's school behaviour. However, there are other factors which could underpin persistent unwanted behaviour.

Towards personal autonomy

The overall aim of any approach to managing behaviour is to enable children to take responsibility for their own behaviour and actions. The strategies outlined are offered with this in mind. The way questions are phrased, interactions conducted and learning opportunities managed contribute to children's developing awareness of their own personal autonomy. For example, subtle changes in phrasing convey significantly different messages. Consider the following statements, designed to encourage children to finish their work:

(a) 'As soon as you have finished your work you can go out to play.'
(b) 'If you don't finish your work you will not be able to go out to play.'

In the former, the teacher tells the children what they have to do before they go out. This gives them responsibility and carries the implication that the children have a choice about whether they complete their work. In the second statement the underlying message is very different. The teacher sets himself or herself up as the person who will deny children the opportunity to play if work is not completed. Through helping children to appreciate the benefits of learning and the consequences of their actions, teachers encourage children to make their own choices about their future learning and behaviour.

This chapter has described a positive system of behaviour management, which focuses on teachers' expectations for children's behaviour, and on how to facilitate this through encouragement and praise rather than criticism and punishment. It aims to enable children to appreciate the impact of their behaviour on others and to recognize that there are more pleasing and desirable ways of fulfilling personal goals and of gaining teacher attention and peer approval than misbehaviour.

Teachers also have to recognize the limits of their influence.

They do not have the training or expertise to delve deeply into children's family backgrounds and patterns of interaction. Their skills lie in successfully organizing the classroom environment to provide experiences which are sensitive to previous learning and which promote changes where appropriate in children's social interactions.

Generally, reference has been made in this chapter to teachers' role in *managing*, rather than *controlling*, classroom behaviour. The processes discussed have focused on the role of teachers as 'managers' of the social environment. Although the effects of successful 'classroom control' and 'management' may be the same, the intent and underlying philosophies are different. Autonomy and personal responsibility are the more likely outcomes of a learning environment based on a philosophy of management rather than control. Ultimately it will be a teacher's own attitudes, values and beliefs, together with her or his professional skills, that determine children's educational and social development.

Chapter 6

PARENTS, TEACHERS AND CHILDREN: WORKING TOGETHER

Introduction

One of the most significant shifts in emphasis in recent years has been the increasing role given to parents' involvement in their children's education. This chapter explores:

- the current contexts in which parents and teachers collaborate:
- the impact of recent legislative changes;
- key principles for establishing an effective partnership:
- the role of parents within the 1981 Education Act (Special Needs).

Parents have always been seen as crucial to their children's development, but it is recent legislation that has sanctioned their extensive involvement in school life. The changes have increased parental choice over the schools their children attend, and offered them more participation on school governing bodies and, following the 1981 Education Act, greater rights with respect to children with special needs.

In addition, schools have involved parents in collaborative ventures so that they can help to teach their children to read at home. Research conducted in Haringey in the 1970s suggested that children made better progress in reading when parents listened to them read at home on a regular basis. This provided the impetus for parent–teacher projects in reading all over the country. Subsequently, projects have been developed to include the teaching of maths.

Such parent–teacher collaborations have been established practice for some time within special education. Many local education authorities in the United Kingdom use the Portage project for the pre-school physically handicapped. Portage is a programme of activities to be undertaken at home by parents following consultation with health visitors, educational psychologists or specially appointed Portage workers. The original Portage materials have been adapted in many LEAs so that parental interventions are geared to their own needs and circumstances.

The changing involvement of parents

Recent legislation highlights the changing relationships between parents and schools. In the past, education has often been viewed as a series of partnerships. Central government worked in tandem with local government, which in turn was in partnership with its schools. Schools, in turn, forged partnerships with parents, on the understanding that this was in the interests of individual children.

With the new legislation, the balance of power has shifted away from local authorities and towards central government and schools. The change in control brings a very different philosophy to bear on how education is to be conducted in the future. In the past, central and local government planned as best they could to provide a system of education that attempted to be egalitarian in nature. The aim was to provide equality of opportunity, and government determined how best to allocate resources to achieve this. LEAs had flexibility over how they funded the education service and could offer support to those schools that experienced difficulties in meeting children's needs. In principle at least, LEAs could assist schools in making the best possible provision for the children under their care. Schools are now funded largely in terms of how many pupils they have on their roll, with very little scope for LEAs to resource specific schools according to their needs.

The concept of partnership and planning is now replaced with that of the 'market place'. Parents rather than children have become the consumers of the education services. It is thus envisaged that parents will shop around and look for the best buy. Parents also have power as a group to vote for their child's school to seek grant-maintained status – to opt out of LEA control and to be funded directly by the DES.

These measures attempt to make schools accountable for the service they provide. It is argued that parents will continue to send their children to schools that 'perform well' and to seek alternatives to those which do not. It is further argued that competition between schools for pupils will lead to an improvement in academic standards. The 'good' schools will flourish and those that are deemed 'less good' will have fewer pupils and become less viable.

How do parents assess schools?

Are parents going to be seduced into examining the first reported assessments and conclude that those schools which gain the best outcomes are the most effective? A number of recent publications have outlined the dangers of relying on final reported outcomes, since they take no account of children's prior knowledge or achievements and do not reflect progress made over time, which it is necessary to know in order to determine a school's effectiveness. This issue was discussed in Chapter 4. While parents may judge schools on published SAT results, it is likely that other factors will also be considered. The nature of a school's links with home, the children's response to learning, their enthusiasm for school, their attitudes and comments about teachers will all help parents to make decisions about a school's effectiveness.

Accepting responsibility

Much of what might be said about parents and teachers is thrown into sharp focus when it is felt that a child is experiencing a difficulty. It is not uncommon for either party to feel defensive in the face of perceived, even if not actual, criticism. Some research into teachers' views on the nature of children's difficulties implies that they are likely to suggest that it is due to the child's home background, particularly in the case of behaviour problems, or that there is something wrong with the child. This is not an encouraging basis for parent–teacher collaborations.

When children experience difficulties in learning, teachers may feel privately that their lack of expertise might have contributed to the current problems. Professionally, this is quite threatening, and it is tempting to accept that the home background or the characteristics of the child are the more significant factors in leading to the difficulties. If a teacher does not accept any responsibility, where does this leave any future collaborations with parents? A teacher who adopts this starting point in discussions with parents effectively implies:

- 'There is something wrong with your child.'
- 'The home environment is largely responsible for the child's difficulties.'
- 'I am not responsible for your child's difficulties.'

It is unlikely that a constructive relationship would start from this beginning.

Teachers are likely to feel uncomfortable and apprehensive about acknowledging to parents that school could be contributing to a child's difficulties. The teacher who is able to say to parents 'I feel your child is experiencing difficulties in learning/behaviour, etc. and I feel uncomfortable with this, because we have not achieved the success we would have liked' is creating the possibility of a more open interaction in the future. As professionals, the onus is on teachers to develop a successful home–school partnership to help children who are experiencing difficulties.

Acknowledging the concerns of parents

There are many occasions when parents voice their concerns to teachers over their children's progress. It is not uncommon for parents to be told 'Not to worry, Jane is making good progress' or 'Yes, Michael has had some problems, but he will grow out of them . . .'. Even where teachers feel that parental concerns are premature and without substance, such responses effectively undermine the parents' perceptions and do not acknowledge their concerns.

Similarly, teachers report that certain parents are unwilling to accept that their child is experiencing any difficulties. This is unfortunate but does not prevent the teacher from instigating whatever measures are appropriate in his or her professional judgement. Teachers are likely to be seen as knowledgeable over the nature of children's difficulties and the teaching of literacy and numeracy skills, but whatever a teacher's insights into children, parents will have an equally deep, albeit on occasions different, understanding of their own children.

Parents and teachers come into contact in a number of different situations and on many occasions during the school year, but these are typically initiated by the school rather than by parents. Although this is changing, it is still schools that determine the form, frequency and timings of contact. Parents want to know about their children's progress and teachers want to inform them when they feel a child is experiencing difficulties. This has to be set in the context of the usual pattern of contact between the two. Parents are likely to be more receptive if there is a background of positive interactions. It is not enough to state that difficulties exist, as this does not necessarily imply that a course of action is going to be pursued to overcome them. Where statements of concern are concluded with positive initiatives to deal with the problems, parents are likely to be more supportive to any proposed solutions.

Collaborative working

An effective collaboration can be seen to develop from teachers conveying respect, empathy and genuineness to parents.

Conveying respect. Successful collaborative ventures between parents and teachers require a good deal of trust, and an understanding that both parties are motivated with the best of intentions and have an effective contribution to make in resolving difficulties. Parents and teachers have different responsibilities, and a meeting where parents recognize that they are seen as equals helps to establish a positive basis for discussion.

Respect is also conveyed by what is known as 'active listening'. We often think of listening as a passive process but, in reality, it involves communicating to a speaker that you are listening through appropriate non-verbal behaviour, feeding back what you have heard and checking you have correctly understood what the speaker intended to say.

The nature of the initial contact sets the scene for any collaborative activities. How was time negotiated with parents? How were parents received on arriving at school? Did the meeting start promptly? Were they offered cups of tea or coffee? It is often many of the 'little things' that do most to enhance or damage a parent's perceptions of school. The combined effect of such overtures creates a positive atmosphere for parent–teacher relationships and helps parents to appreciate that their presence is valued.

Conveying empathy. Establishing empathy involves placing ourselves in someone else's shoes in order to gain an appreciation of their perceptions and understanding of the world. It is conveyed not so much by saying 'I understand' or 'I can imagine how you feel' as by indicating to parents that you understand how they are feeling. It is an application of active listening, but relates specifically to parents' feelings and emotions rather than more general conversational topics.

Being genuine. Genuineness is usually conveyed through teachers being willing to disclose something of their own experiences or feelings during conversations with parents. Appropriate self-disclosure is not so much exchanging anecdotes ('If you think you've got problems . . .', etc.) as indicating that you have appreciated how they are feeling. It is intended to convey that it is all right to feel as they do and that such feelings are an understandable response to events.

Having outlined the basic interpersonal principles behind successful collaborations, this section now explores two strands which have emerged in collaborative work with parents. The first is joint parent–teacher ventures, in which parents work directly with their children in tandem with teachers to help promote learning. The second involves the various support and advisory which exist within education, health and social service departments.

Collaborating with children's learning

Parental involvement in children's learning is now relatively well established in the field of special education. Educational psychologists and teachers of severely mentally or physically handicapped children have run projects over a number of years to involve parents actively in their children's learning.

Parents are of course inevitably involved in their children's learning. The environment they create has a major impact on learning. Some children have already started to learn to read before they start school, and the process of parental help continues through listening to them reading a book sent home from school and going through selected sight vocabulary sent home in word tins. Where many projects targeted on children with difficulties differed was that they often grew from concerns about children's reading progress, and they attempted to involve parents in a slightly more formal and structured manner than had hitherto been the case.

A number of projects were first initiated by groups of educational psychologists rather than schools. These projects often grew from the individual casework being undertaken by the psychologist. Parents indicated a willingness to do anything possible to help promote their children's learning. Other parents within the school then wanted similar help and schools agreed to set up their own parent–teacher reading projects.

The many projects have varied enormously in their scope and in the demands placed on parents. In some cases, parents' principal role was to listen to children read on a regular basis and to record their progress. In others, parents were actually given systematic guidance in teaching every aspect of reading and collaborated in a comprehensive way with school. Many children who were initially seen to have difficulties in learning to read benefited enormously from the help they received from their parents.

What are the implications for the role parents are being asked to take, particularly in relation to children experiencing difficulties, and our concept of the 'good parent'? It has already been stated that many parents have involved themselves, albeit on a voluntary basis, in their children's formal learning at school. Now there is an expectation that they will be involved if requested by the school. Can parents say 'No' to any involvement in projects without their role as parents being impugned? Can they still be regarded as supportive, caring parents if they do not want to take part in a home–school reading project? What is the response to parents who reasonably claim they have neither the time nor the expertise to take part, that there are other things they want to do with their children and that they expect the 'experts' to teach their child to read?

To continue: would parents expressing these or similar views be seen to be neglecting their parental responsibilities? Might they be regarded as unsupportive and uninterested in their children's education? Is the request for parents to become involved in a project a genuine invitation or an implied demand?

Education, health and social support services

The collaboration between parents and teachers is often seen to be at the heart of successful learning, but other professional groups may be involved where there are perceived difficulties. A range of professionals from education (such as educational psychologists, advisory teachers of the visually or hearing impaired), health (clinical psychologists, speech therapists, school medical officers, general practitioners, psychiatrists) and social services (social workers) offer support, advice and guidance to parents, teachers and children.

The Warnock Report proposed a five-stage model of assessment which provided for the gradual involvement of support services. When the 1981 Education Act first came into force, the government circular accompanying its introduction endorsed the view that LEA assessment procedures 'should allow for the progressive extension of professional involvement from the class teacher to the headteacher, a specialist teacher, the educational psychologist, the school doctor and nurse and other professionals in the education, health and social services' (DES, 1983).

This section on support services explores some of the issues created by the involvement of various professional groups and examines some of the potential professional tensions which can emerge. The discussion will first of all consider referrals to psychiatrists and psychologists. Similar issues exist for most of the major support services.

It is helpful to clarify the distinction between psychiatrists and psychologists. Psychiatrists are doctors who receive training in general psychiatry before possibly specializing in child psychiatry. Psychologists are not doctors and have no medical training. There are two main professional groups of psychologists working with children – clinical and educational. Clinical psychologists are employed by the health service and educational psychologists by LEAs, although this may change in the future. All three groups overlap considerably in terms of their professional involvement. This can create tensions between them, but they often confront similar issues when working with children, parents and teachers.

Child psychiatry and psychology are quite different from other branches of psychiatry and psychology. In adult psychiatry or psychology, it is usually the adults who recognize that they have problems in their lives and seek professional help to address them. In the areas of child psychiatry and psychology, although the children are seen to have the problem, they do not refer themselves. The problems they present are invariably identified and articulated by someone other than the child, usually a parent or teacher. They see the child has a problem and so expect the professionals to effect a cure, which is directed towards the child.

In earlier chapters, there was discussion of the extent to which problems can arise through the way children interact within their environments. The contexts in which problems emerge then become the focus of intervention, not just the child. Thus, for many psychiatrists and psychologists, the starting point is not the child but the referring agent. The initial focus is on understanding why the child is seen to have a problem, and for this it is necessary to appreciate the perceptions and motives of the parent or teacher who first identifies the problem. The intervention which follows may then involve the whole family in examining their behaviour, or a teacher in exploring the nature of his or her involvement with children, on a broader basis than strictly in relation to the child with problems.

Examining the contexts in which difficulties occur and exploring the perceptions of those involved raises a number of issues. Parents or teachers are unlikely to welcome any suggestion that they may be part of the problem, and may be hostile to the idea that their perceptions and behaviour need to be considered in any overall analysis of the difficulties. Historically, diagnosis and treatment have taken place in a neutral environment. In recent times interventions are more likely to occur in the settings in which problems occur. This, then, is likely to lead to an increase in visits and periods of observation and discussion in the home and school.

The above issues also have implications for the other support services identified earlier. Where a child is partially sighted, blind, partially hearing or deaf, these circumstances will affect other family members. The problems caused by these conditions have to be addressed by all the family, not just the child who experiences them.

Many support services advise others on how to manage problems rather than dealing with them directly themselves. So a psychiatrist may work with other health workers; educational psychologists will organize in-service courses for teachers, discuss areas of concern and then debate various forms of intervention. It is an effective use of time. For example, one hour spent on an in-service course with 30 teachers can have an impact on the learning experiences of a large number of children – more than if the psychologist saw teachers individually. Many education, health and social support services intervene and collaborate with teachers and parents within the working relationships outlined.

The 1981 Education Act and parental involvement

The 1981 Education Act gave parents a more central role in the decision-making process about their children's education. Schools and LEAs were exhorted to involve parents at the earliest opportunity in the assessment process. The Act also required that parents be consulted before initiating a formal, statutory assessment. Parents may make their own independent representations to the LEA, offering their own views on their children's educational needs.

All professionals submitting advice to LEAs have to consult parents and take into account their opinions. Also, whenever feasible, parents are permitted to attend any assessments carried out on their children. This assumes that an assessment of children's educational needs takes place as a one-off event on a limited number of occasions and is likely to be associated with the normative and psychometric approaches to assessment discussed in Chapter 3. It is less practical for parents to attend where assessment is seen as a continuous process. In this case, parents can be fully informed of their children's progress and participate with teachers in establishing and working towards agreed educational goals.

Parents receive copies of all the advice sent to the director of education, and when a provisional statement is drafted, they have to approve its contents before it can become substantive. Where parents are unhappy with the statement's contents, they can appeal to an LEA committee and ultimately to the Secretary of State for Education. They can also appeal against an LEA decision not to issue a statement. In the former case the Secretary of State is empowered to direct the LEA to change some aspect of its decision. In the latter case this is not so, and the most that parents can expect is that the Secretary of State will direct an LEA to reconsider its decision; it cannot be directed to change. Finally, it must be noted that details of existing legislation may change in the future.

Although parents have been given increased rights under the 1981 Education Act, many parents are not in a position to exercise those rights. LEA documentation is not always readily understood. Teachers and psychologists who are LEA employees may feel constrained at times to make recommendations which comply with local authority wishes rather than representing the best interests of the child. The language associated with the legislation can be seen by parents as full of jargon and difficult to follow.

While parents have rights, the onus is now on them to take the initiative. Many parents may feel overwhelmed at the prospect of negotiating their way through the complicated paperwork, detailed procedures and LEA hierarchies in order to press home their case. Studies examining the extent to which LEAs are prepared to statement children requiring special educational needs suggest that there is some reluctance to do so because of the resource implications. Alternatively, some authorities have issued statements but do not currently have the resources to make appropriate provision. Parents and children are expected to wait until these become available. There are also cases where the LEA has suggested that fewer formal statutory assessments will be made. This denies parents their legal right to an assessment, which they are entitled to request.

Despite this negative portrayal of some LEAs, it must be recognized that they are in an unenviable position, as they have limited resources. There is another factor that has probably contributed to the increase in requests for formal statutory assessments. Prior to the implementation of the 1981 Education Act, LEA support services and particularly educational psychologists were increasingly engaged in preventive work through in-service training of teachers and courses for parents of the sort described at the end of the previous section. In this way teachers became increasingly confident and competent to manage a range of problems.

Working with teachers meant that fewer children were

referred to educational psychological services, which led to a substantial decline in waiting lists. Unfortunately the momentum behind much of the advisory work has been lost since the 1981 Education Act was introduced.

Over time, the impact of the 1981 Act has increased the demand for psychologists to work directly with children, and there are fewer opportunities to run in-service courses. Although some LEAs have recognized the value of preventive work being undertaken by psychologists, far less is taking place in the 1990s than was happening in the early part of the 1980s. In recent times the professional journals of educational psychologists have focused far more on the individual assessment of children than on the details of preventive in-service work.

Research undertaken into the extent and manner in which the 1981 Education Act has been implemented by LEAs has tended to suggest that the optimism generated at its inception was somewhat misplaced. The learning opportunities of children and the experiences of many parents indicate that there is still some way to go before the spirit of the Act can be seen to have been fully acknowledged and implemented by LEAs.

This chapter has discussed the present contexts in which parents and teachers collaborate. Parents are increasingly seen as consumers within the education system, and so it is important that parents and teachers establish an effective rapport with each other. This is more likely to occur within a relationship based on trust and a recognition that both parties are concerned to secure successful outcomes for children. Parents and teachers may well feel defensive in the face of perceived criticism over the nature of children's difficulties, but where these are acknowledged, the basis for making a collaborative response to overcoming problems is established.

CONCLUSION: WHAT IS SPECIAL EDUCATION?

This section highlights recurring themes which provide the basis for meeting children's educational needs.

Examining assumptions

At any time, the political, social and economic climate creates the context in which certain educational practices and beliefs are likely to find favour. The beginning of the 1990s has seen education feature prominently as a political issue. There has rarely been a time when teaching methods and standards have not occupied the thoughts of politicians and teachers. Teachers who are able to retain a sense of direction and examine the assumptions on which changes are advocated are better able to maintain their perspective, and to bring a critical awareness to their evaluation of existing or suggested practice.

Labels

Over the years we have become increasingly aware of the potential dangers of labelling children. While we categorize aspects of our personal worlds to bring order and cohesion to our lives, the tendency to do this in relation to special education should be resisted. We have shown ourselves to be increasingly sophisticated in our use of labels over the years. Could it be that the 'imbeciles' and 'idiots' of past legislation are now the children we categorize as having special educational needs? We may claim that our perceptions of children's competencies are not affected by such labels, but research suggests that this is unlikely.

Meeting educational needs

In any class of children, teachers have to meet a variety of educational needs. Inevitably some children will make better progress than others, irrespective of how their learning is organized. There will always be a tendency to believe that those who achieve less than peers might do so because of a difficulty in learning. We are less likely to assume this if we recognize that any group of children will have a range of attainments. The teacher's role is to facilitate children's future learning, *regardless of their current attainments*. Whether standards are falling or are the same or are improving is not the issue. The question to be addressed is how to develop and promote children's learning, given their existing skills, knowledge and experience.

Teacher expectations

The 1960s and 1970s generated a considerable amount of research on the importance of maintaining high expectations for children's learning. More recently, the report by Alexander, Rose and Woodhead (DES, 1992) noted the need for teachers to have high expectations for children's progress. While this is clearly known by the majority if not by all teachers, it is a principle that is not readily translated into practice. Chapter 2 in particular drew attention to the potentially harmful effects of making reference to children's abilities. The personal histories we bring to teaching often mean that we have preconceived notions of how children learn and behave with respect to their gender, race, social class or current attainments.

Teaching in such diverse contexts as those of Project Follow Through in the USA (for children with learning difficulties) and of children with cerebral palsy at the Peto Institute (through conductive education) illustrate how even the most apparently intractable problems can be overcome to some extent. It is reported that brain-damaged English children who are taught at the Peto Institute have become fluent in Hungarian. If this is so, what might the implication be for other children? What is the equivalent step in learning for all those children in our schools who are not brain-damaged but are seen to be having difficulties in learning to read? Accepting the importance of high expectations is unlikely to be sufficient to make a significant difference to children's learning if the factors which constrain progress, such as perceptions of children's ability and potential learning, are not also addressed.

Collaborative teaching

The introduction of the 1988 Education Act has required teachers to work together closely to plan how to meet its requirements. Individual teachers may feel that their professional expertise is threatened when children are experiencing difficulties. However, problems can more readily be overcome where the expertise of colleagues is shared through collaborative working.

Developing a policy

Where teachers, schools and LEAs work collaboratively to develop policies on special needs, available resources can be maximized. HMI reports have made reference to this. For example, HMI stated in *A Survey of Pupils with Special Needs in Ordinary Schools* (DES, 1989b):

> In the past few years about half the schools visited had reviewed their identification and monitoring procedures, organisation, classroom practice and staff training fur pupils with SEN. In almost all these schools a whole school policy for SEN had been developed. Where this involved all school staff, was actively supported by the school's senior management, and was properly co-ordinated by an appropriately experienced and qualified teacher, it had a positive effect on the quality of work from pupils with SEN. (para. 3)

The Elton Committee's report on *Discipline in Schools* (DES, 1989a) also recommended that 'headteachers should, in consultation with the governors, develop whole school behaviour policies which are clearly understood by pupils, parents and other school staff' (para. 51). The committee outlined features of a policy, some of which are:

- the policy should be based on a clear and defensible set of principles or values (para. 53);

- behaviour policies should be specific to each school (para. 54);
- headteachers and teachers should ensure that rules are applied consistently by all members of staff (para. 58);
- it should be clear that the principles of the behaviour policy apply to all school activities on or off site;
- it is the job of the headteacher and senior management team of a school to monitor the way in which the behaviour is working.

Schools make a difference

A number of major research initiatives in recent years have indicated that some schools are more effective than others. Similarly, within any school some teachers are likely to be more effective than others. Increasingly the factors which contribute to a school's and teacher's effectiveness are being identified. Many have been introduced in this book and others will undoubtedly emerge in the coming months and years, as debates and research into teacher effectiveness continue.

Problem solving

There are no miracle cures for changing well-established learning and behaviour patterns. A problem-solving approach allows teachers to maintain their autonomy and resist the whims of fashion, by providing a framework which systematically assesses and evaluates children's learning and the effectiveness of teaching.

Being a 'good enough' teacher

A phrase frequently repeated in books and magazines for parents is the need to accept being a 'good enough' parent, rather than striving for the unobtainable ideal of being the 'perfect' parent. There are parallels for teachers. A recurring theme in this book has been for teachers to accept responsibility for children's learning. However, they do not teach in a vacuum and there are constraints in various aspects of their professional lives. While acknowledging other factors that impinge on classroom practice, it is argued in this book that teachers must organize the resources at their disposal as effectively as possible. They must accept that doing their best is 'good enough'.

Attitudes, values and beliefs

It is not always easy to retain a sense of direction and purpose when faced with the number of changes currently being introduced into the education system. There have been times in the past when children's failure has been blamed on the children themselves, their parents, society at large or, as is the current trend, teachers and schools. Urging teachers to take responsibility for children's learning is not yet another attack on teachers' competences. What is seen to be important in determining what children learn is the attitudes, values and beliefs not only of teachers but of all those responsible for educating children.

Redefining special education

The 1981 Education Act provides a legal framework for determining which children have special educational needs, and the steps to be followed in securing appropriate provision to meet those needs. I would like to conclude this book by further defining what I believe characterizes 'special education'. Education becomes special when it:

- examines perceptions of children's learning which may create barriers to their progress;
- assumes children can learn;
- generates hypotheses about how to overcome difficulties;
- provides a framework within which to teach and promote children's learning;
- makes a difference to children's lives in terms of their learning outcomes and life opportunities.

REFERENCES

Audit Commission and HMI (1992), *Getting in on the Act: provision for pupils with special educational needs: the national picture* (HMSO, London).

N. Bennett, C. Desforges, A. Cockburn and B. Wilkinson (1984), *The Quality of Pupil Learning Experiences* (Lawrence Erlbaum Associates, London).

S. L. Bull and J. E. Solity (1987), *Classroom Management: principles to practice* (Croom Helm, London).

P. Croll and D. Moses (1985), *One in Five: the assessment and incidence of special educational needs* (Routledge and Kegan Paul, London).

DES (1978), *Special Educational Needs* (The Warnock Report) (HMSO, London).

DES (1980), *Education Act* (HMSO, London).

DES (1981), *Education Act* (HMSO, London).

DES (1982), *Mathematics Counts* (The Cockcroft Report) (HMSO, London).

DES (1983), *Assessments and Statements of Special Educational Needs* (Circular 1/83) (HMSO, London).

DES (1988), *Education Reform Act* (HMSO, London).

DES (1989a), *Discipline in Schools* (The Elton Report) (HMSO, London).

DES (1989b), *A Survey of Pupils with Special Needs in Ordinary Schools* (HMSO, London).

DES (1990), *Aspects of Primary Education: the teaching and learning of language and literacy* (HMSO, London).

DES (1992), *Curriculum Organization and Classroom Practice in Primary Schools: a discussion paper* (HMSO, London).

C. Gipps, H. Gross and H. Goldstein (1987), *Warnock's Eighteen Per Cent: children with special needs in the primary school* (Falmer Press, Lewes).

N. G. Haring and M. D. Eaton (1978), 'Systematic instructional procedures: an instructional hierarchy' in N. G. Haring *et al.* (eds), *The Fourth R: research in the classroom* (Charles E. Merrill, Columbus, Ohio).

NCC (National Curriculum Council) (1989a), *Implementing the National Curriculum: participation by pupils with special educational needs* (Circular no. 5, May) (NCC, York).

NCC (National Curriculum Council) (1989b), *A Curriculum for All: special educational needs in the National Curriculum* (NCC, York).

N. Postman and C. Weingartner (1969), *Teaching as a Subversive Activity* (Penguin, Harmondsworth).

SEAC (School Examinations and Assessment Council) (1989), *A Guide to Teacher Assessment (Pack C): a source book of teacher assessment* (SEAC, London).

SEAC (School Examinations and Assessment Council) (1992), *Suggested Guidelines for a More Standardised Approach to Number (and Number Notation) in Teacher Assessment* (SEAC, London).

J. E. Solity and S. L. Bull (1987), *Special Needs: bridging the curriculum gap* (Open University Press, Buckingham).

J. E. Solity and E. C. Raybould (1988), *A Teacher's Guide to Special Needs: a positive response to the 1981 Education Act* (Open University Press, Buckingham).

FURTHER READING

Issues in special education

T. Dessent (1989), *Making the Ordinary School Special* (Falmer Press, Lewes).

B. Norwich (1990), *Reappraising Special Needs Education* (Cassell, London).

G. Thomas and A. Feiler (eds) (1988), *Planning for Special Needs: a whole school approach* (Blackwell, Oxford).

Special education and the law

ACE (Advisory Centre for Education) (5th edition, 1992), *The Law on Children with Special Needs* (ACE, London).

J. E. Solity and E. C. Raybould (1988), *A Teacher's Guide to Special Needs: a positive response to the 1981 Education Act* (Open University Press, Buckingham).

Children with learning difficulties

M. Ainscow and J. Muncey (1989), *Meeting Individual Needs* (David Fulton, London).

D. W. Carnine and J. Silbert (1979), *Direct Instruction Reading* (Charles E. Merrill, Columbus, Ohio).

Working with parents

K. Topping and S. Wolfendale (1985), *Parental Involvement in Children's Reading* (Croom Helm, London).

S. Wolfendale *et al.* (1993), *Empowering Parents and Teachers: working for children* (Cassell, London).

Research into special educational needs

N. Bennett and A. Cass (1989), *From Special to Ordinary Schools: case studies in integration* (Cassell, London).

P. Croll and D. Moses (1985), *One in Five: the assessment and incidence of special educational needs* (Routledge and Kegan Paul, London).

C. Gipps, H. Gross and H. Goldstein (1987), *Warnock's Eighteen Per Cent: children with special needs in the primary school* (Falmer Press, Lewes).

D. Moses, S. Hegarty and S. Jowett (1988), *Supporting Ordinary Schools: L.E.A. initiatives* (NFER-Nelson, Windsor).

Legislation related to children with special needs

DES (1981), *Education Act* (HMSO, London).

DES (1988), *Eduction Reform Act* (HMSO, London).

DES (1989), *Assessments and Statements of Special Educational Needs: procedures within education, health and social services* (Circular 22/89) (HMSO, London).

DES (1991), *Local Management of Schools: further guidance* (Circular 7/91) (HMSO, London).

Reports on special education

Audit Commission and HMI (1992), *Getting in on the Act: provision for pupils with special educational needs: the national picture* (HMSO, London).

DES (1978), *Special Educational Needs* (The Warnock Report) (HMSO, London).

DES (1989a), *Discipline in Schools* (The Elton Report) (HMSO, London).

DES (1989b), *A Survey of Pupils with Special Needs in Ordinary Schools* (HMSO, London).

DES (1990), *Special Needs Issues* (HMSO, London).

NCC (National Curriculum Council) (1989), *A Curriculum For All: special educational needs in the National Curriculum* (NCC, York).

Journals covering topics in special education

British Journal of Special Education
Educational Psychology
Educational Psychology in Practice
European Journal of Special Needs Education
Special Children
Support for Learning

INDEX

ability   33–4
assessment   6, 9, 18–19, 21–2,
   52–3, 56, 59–82
   aims   60–1
   assessment-through-
      teaching   70–7
   criterion-referenced   61, 63,
      65, 72
   involving children   72
   ipsative   61, 63–4, 65
   key stages   59, 64, 77–9
   normative   61–3, 65, 70
   standard assessment
      tasks   77–9, 110
   statutory assessment
      procedure   79–81
   teacher assessment   64–79
   see also precision teaching
assessment-through-
   teaching   70–7

behaviour   83–108
   control   107
   criticism trap   102–3
   developing personal
      autonomy   106
   influence of family
      background   86–91
   managing classroom
      behaviour   91–107
   nature of classroom
      behaviour   84–6
   non-verbal behaviour   93–5,
      103
   responding to children's
      behaviour   97–9
   responding to unwanted
      behaviour   102–5
   teacher expectations   95–7
   teacher status   92, 94
   understanding unwanted
      behaviour   99–102

behavioural objectives   53–4,
   65–9, 76
beliefs   2
Burt, Cyril   4, 26

child-centred education   7,
   8–10, 50, 53, 56
criticism trap   102–3
curriculum   47–8, 50–2
   see also National Curriculum
Curriculum for All, A   35–6, 44

direct instruction   50, 51

Education Act 1870   3
Education Act 1944   4, 5
Education Act 1980   21
Education (Special Needs) Act
   1981   6, 15, 16, 17, 20, 21, 36,
   59, 79, 108, 115–16, 118–20,
   125
Education Reform Act 1988   7,
   21, 51, 59, 123
educational needs   35–7, 52
educational psychologists   5,
   15, 18, 43, 80, 81, 109, 114, 115,
   116, 117, 119, 120
Elton Committee   91, 101–2,
   123

feedback   55, 56, 76

governors   22

handicap   2–7, 14

instructional hierarchy   54–6,
   57
integration   6, 20
intelligence   4, 5, 6, 9, 26–7, 59,
   74

Kelly, George   99